Peers in the Classroom
Case Studies in Adult Higher Education

edited by

Regina Lopata Logan

& Robert Fromberg

Northwestern University
University College
Evanston, Illinois   60208

*Although based on authors' experiences, these cases
do not represent actual people or events.*

 **NEW FORUMS PRESS** INC.
Stillwater, Oklahoma

Printed in the United States of America.

Additional copies may be ordered from New Forums Press,
Inc., P.O. Box 876, Stillwater, OK 74076; or, by phone at
(405) 372-6158. Visit our web site at www.newforums.com.

ISBN: 1-58107-013-6

Peers in the Classroom
Case Studies in Adult Higher Education

Table of Contents

Part I: Adult Higher Education and the Use of Case Studies

Faculty who teach adults need to model lifelong learning. Case studies are a particularly effective tool to encourage students along this path. When using cases with faculty who teach adults, the principles of adult learning are as effective as they are with adult students.

This essay defines and describes case studies, examines the appeal and power of case studies, and explains what problems they address and how they help the cause of improved teaching and learning. Current use of cases on various campuses is included.

An unusual aspect of Northwestern's University College Faculty Development Program is the inclusion of students in two case discussions each year. This approach affords the opportunity for direct interaction between students and faculty. The dynamic is especially intriguing because the students are adults and thus age peers with (if not older than) the faculty. At the outset of the case discussion, it is often unclear who is a student and who is an instructor. This ambiguity allows for a certain anonymity, which leads to very open, frank discussions. The result is that students and faculty get insights into each others' perspectives that they would not have in any other situation.

Part II: Cases from a Faculty Perspective

The following cases present classroom issues from the perspective of faculty members, such as teaching students who are well read and vocal, who juggle studies with busy professional and personal lives, who are nervous about returning to the university, and who may unintentionally inject an unusual social dynamic into the classroom because they are the same age as, or older than, the instructors.

A veteran English faculty member, Luther is well regarded for his skilled teaching. However, he may have become somewhat opinionated over the years. Darcy Herbst, angry and resentful, is struggling to complete her degree. She finds Luther to be biased, racist, and antifeminist, and she is out to teach him a lesson.

Because of his learning disability, Stuart frequently requests special considerations, especially pertaining to exams. The instructor of his evening class is willing to comply, but becomes skeptical when Stuart's specifications are always issued at the last minute and border on the excessive. The instructor begins to feel he is being taken advantage of and wonders about the fairness of the situation to other students.

Belinda is a well-read adult student pursuing a degree in the evening division of a large university. In a literary theory class, Belinda refuses to read the required material. She labels it misogynist and tells the class that by reading it, they are encouraging sexism. Her attitude challenges the authority of the instructor and the relevance of the class material.

Carsi Richards Hughes

As a first-time teacher, the twenty-five-year old graduate student is eager for her class of adults to like her. She is especially concerned that her youth will be a stumbling block for the students who are between 26 and 62. Early in the semester, she receives a love letter from one of her students. She becomes concerned that her teaching style and attitude encouraged this infatuation, but is also upset at the unsolicited attention.

Robert Fromberg

Instructor Paul Hughes, an adjunct faculty member for an evening university program, takes an instant dislike to Jennifer, a student whose harried manner he finds extremely annoying. The situation is further complicated by Jennifer's poor performance in class, which she explains are due to the stress of being a single working mother with her own business. Paul struggles to determine if his personal dislike of Jennifer is coloring his ability to treat the student fairly.

Laurence D. Schiller

Mike, a student auditing a class on the Middle East, is a frequent disturbance in class. His behavior is confrontational and sarcastic, and he continually draws class discussion away from the topic to voice his opinion. The instructor wonders how to deflect the student without hindering the discussion format of the classroom.

Kurt Cogswell

The summer calculus course is intense, meeting for three hours an evening, five nights a week. To make the material more manageable, the teacher divides the class into small groups. One group, consisting of a mix of traditional and nontraditional aged students, has difficulty keeping pace, and the instructor spends the majority of his time working with them. At the end of the session, he wonders how he might have changed the group dynamic to make it function more effectively.

Robert Fromberg

A women's studies instructor has had success beginning her day-school classes by showing a videotape of the pop star Madonna as a way to start a discussion about women and society. In an evening class populated by adult students, however, an older woman is offended by the videotape and presents an articulate complaint to the dean.

> *Pam, a student returning to earn her degree after an eleven-year absence from a university setting, has doubts about her ability to succeed in an English composition class. The instructor offers his assistance, but soon feels that the student is demanding too much of his attention. By the middle of the fourteen-week semester, Pam has requested weekly consultations, leaving the instructor to question the limits of a teacher's responsibility to an individual student, and wondering what options he should have considered to assist a nervous returning student.*

> *In a small composition class, the dynamic is affected by Ralph, a very vocal student. Ralph frequently expresses his dislike of the essays in a dismissive tone that causes the other students to question the material. Michael, the instructor, must deal with this intimidating older man who is taking control of his class.*

> *Erica teaches a course for returning adult students. Jane, one of the students in her interpersonal conflict management course, often disrupts class with tirades concerning personal issues. Her outbursts disrupt the class and arrest classroom discussion. Erica senses the class' discomfort, but is unsure of how to gain control of the situation.*

Part III: Cases from a Student Perspective

These cases raise several key issues experienced by adult students. The problems include negotiating with teachers who may be relatively inexperienced, who may not fully understand the demands on a working student, and who may seem not to appreciate the range of ages and experiences among adult students.

> *When Mary, a student just returned to the university after a ten-year absence, earns a C on her first midterm exam, she is devastated. She is further agitated when she discovers that her friend received an A, even*

*though their answers were essentially the same. Mary confronts Ms.
Carne. As Mary points out the correct answers on her exam, the teacher
becomes increasingly less responsive, but finally gives her an A,
although grudgingly. For the remainder of the class, Mary feels
uncomfortable with Ms. Carne and ponders how to deal with this
problem.*

*Jean Greenwood is a student returning to college with some trepidation,
due to a few years absence and previous negative experiences in school.
Robert Holmes, her English instructor, begins the class by teaching the
technicalities of composition, which Jean finds difficult to follow. Later
in the class, his expectations seem to change, requiring the writing to be
more creative. Jean is bewildered, and her performance deteriorates. She
drops the class, and Robert is unsure of what he did to cause such
frustration.*

*Emma Black has been teaching marketing for a number of years. She has
always wanted to assign a group project and decides midway through the
semester that she may as well try it now. She is excited by her creativity
and believes the students will benefit greatly from the opportunity to
have a "real life" experience. The students don't quite see it that way;
they are disgruntled with the assignment as they come up against a
number of obstacles impeding the successful completion of the project.*

*Linda, newly arrived from Australia, enrolls in an evening marketing
class. The first night of class, Linda encounters intense cultural
differences between American and Australian instructors. She finds the
course instructor, Ken Benton, to be arrogant, impatient, and resentful
when she challenges his authority. She fears that the cultural differences
may be too great and considers dropping the course.*

*Michael Bradington, an experienced management consultant and faculty
member, can't seem to appreciate the skills of a homemaker returning to
the classroom. Rita feels devalued and discouraged while Dr. Bradington
thinks he's doing her a favor by giving her a dose of "reality."*

Part IV: Cases from an Administrative Perspective

These cases, three written from the perspective of a dean and one from a faculty developer, present questions of administrative complexity. The deans' cases focus on how and when an administrator should intervene in classroom management and how to handle the various constituents who may be at odds with each other. The faculty developer case looks at the problem of faculty who have traditional notions of how a course should be taught and refuse to consider alternate pedagogical methods.

A distinguished scholar and emeritus professor, Peter Bolonsky, has agreed to teach the capstone seminar for political science majors at University College. His unorthodox teaching methods anger several students who complain bitterly to Dean Carole Sherman. Sherman is in a quandary over whether Bolonsky's approach is too liberal, even sloppy, or the students' expectations too passive and dependent.

Assistant Dean Margaret Smith encounters frequent student complaints about Jennifer, a first-time doctoral teacher in the continuing education division. The students believe that Jennifer expects graduate work from the class, and that she is not presenting the material adequately. Jennifer appears to be receptive to the dean's efforts to correct the situation, but final evaluations reveal that the students remained dissatisfied. Adding to Dean Smith's difficulties, Jennifer pleads with her not to publish the negative evaluations.

Associate Dean Witter faces an adult student charged with plagiarism, which is grounds for dismissal. The student argues that he was not plagiarizing, but borrowing heavily from the CEO letter included in a company's annual report. The dean must decide if the student is guilty, or if he is simply unaccustomed to writing an academic paper, due to his long break from academic life and the lack of written work in his previous courses.

Martha Bowers is the new Coordinator of Faculty Development for the evening division of a university. She arranges a series of workshops on techniques for enhancing classroom discussion. At one seminar, she is confronted with faculty members in the math and science departments who believe the program pointless, as they see lecture as the only suitable method for teaching their courses.

Dedication

For my husband, Pat, and children, Charles, Michael, and Julia, my best teachers, whose support helped me make this book a reality. And, especially, for my wonderful deans, Don Collins and Louise Love, whose patience and trust guided me throughout this project.

—Gina Logan

For Adrianne

—Rob Fromberg

Preface

The genesis of this project was a remark made by a University College student following a faculty-student case study discussion. The student, a professional woman in her early thirties, commented that the case we had been analyzing didn't seem relevant to her. She agreed that the point of the case was generalizable, but the specifics made it seem less feasible to her. It was a case obtained from a prestigious college and it focused on a situation in a course taught by a young teaching assistant to a class of eighteen to twenty-two year old full-time resident students. The University College student pointed out that the situation would seem very different in a classroom where teachers and students were age peers, or where students were older than their teacher, and complicated by issues of commuting, working, and having family obligations. From this student's offhand remark, the idea of a casebook for use in adult education grew into a reality.

We spent many months discussing the idea with faculty, administrators, and students. We asked for contributors and held several writing workshops for all who were interested. The result is in your hands: a collection of twenty cases representing various experiences of faculty, students, and administrators. Although the cases may not represent historical facts, they are all true. We think they convey a sense of the dynamism and complexity that educators of adults and adult students experience when they return to school in the midst of busy adult roles and responsibilities.

We imagine this book will function as a workbook. It is specifically for those involved with adult education. The cases may be used by faculty developers, deans, department chairs, and anyone else who teaches about adults in the classroom. A case may be the focus of a departmental meeting or showcased in a faculty retreat. The cases could be used as part of a course about adult education. However you use the cases, we hope your discussions engender lively debate and insightful reflection.

Regina Lopata Logan
Robert Fromberg
Evanston, Illinois
December 1998

Foreword

Most of us in higher education struggle daily with the need to find more effective ways of meeting the needs of students. Fortunately, we can draw upon a rich literature to enhance our pedagogical strategies and techniques.

But for those of us dedicated to teaching adults older than the students enrolled in traditional university programs, the struggle to effectively reach our students is especially challenging because documented experiences with teaching these students are far from abundant. Moreover, we compete with the intense demands of work and family; many of our students are eager but often tired by the time they arrive at their seats in our classrooms or find the time to study.

Yet the rewards of teaching these students are many. They are highly motivated, and they bring with them extensive experience, significant knowledge, and high standards — both for themselves and for their teachers.

Our dedication to these students, our delight in working with them, and the relative paucity of information about teaching them were all factors that led staff and faculty at University College of Northwestern University to begin collecting case studies in adult education from our faculty, students, and administrators. These cases were intended to provide examples of the barriers and opportunities, missteps and successes that we experience each day as we work with adult students in higher education.

Now that the cases have been edited for inclusion in this volume, we hope that they may achieve a number of intertwined goals:

We hope that they will raise awareness about the singular nature of educating people of this age group.

We hope that they will stimulate discussion about innovative strategies and techniques for engaging adult students in the subjects at hand and in lifelong learning.

We hope that they will show those teaching this age group that they have many partners in this important endeavor.

We hope that they will be a basis for further study and writing about this field.

Doubtless, these case studies, all of which represent edited perceptions of authentic experiences, can be used in various ways. In University College their principal use has been to serve as subjects of informal discussions of an hour or so in length among students and faculty. Given the makeup of the teaching staff and the maturity of the students in the school, a visitor would be hard-pressed to know whether a speaker might be a member of the faculty or a student. Still more striking, however, the nature of a speaker's comments might well offer little clue to his or her identity. Thus, in an adult school, the traditionally sharp differences in the viewpoints of students and faculty can be seen to blur, even to merge. In thirty-five years of working with adult students, I have seen no process more powerful than these discussions at strengthening the common resolve.

We publish these cases with a reminder to our colleagues that the proportion of nontraditional students in higher education is steadily increasing, that this group will shortly eclipse the traditional age group, and that we must continue to work toward understanding the dynamics that operate in adult schools if we are to succeed in our chosen mission.

Donald E. Collins
Dean
University College
Northwestern University
Evanston, Illinois
December 1998

Part I:
Adult Higher Education and the
Use of Case Studies

Using Cases to Promote Adult Learning

Barbara Millis

The literature of adult education has come a long way since Malcolm Knowles first coined the word "androgogy." We now know a great deal about motivating adults, knowledge that faculty developers can put to good use in their role as "change agents." As Wlodkowski (1993) points out, "Most psychologists concerned with learning and education use the word "motivation" to describe those processes that can (a) arouse and instigate behavior, (b) give direction and purpose to behavior, (c) continue to allow behavior to persist, and (d) lead to choosing and preferring a particular behavior" (p. 2).

Faculty developers try to provide faculty with the knowledge and skills to become informed practitioners who deliberately—with reflection—change their classroom behaviors. Few faculty initiate profound changes without the promise of ongoing support; without a firsthand exposure to the technique, either through observation or an experiential workshop; and finally, without the confidence that the projected change will be successful. One of the most useful ways to provide these essential prerequisites is through faculty development cases where faculty grapple firsthand with "real" classroom scenarios. ·

The power of cases, like the power of "stories," has been well documented. They bring immediacy and reality to potentially theoretical material. They stimulate in-depth collaborative problem-solving and thought-provoking, context-specific discussions. Perhaps best of all, they offer opportunities for active, experiential learning. In workshops, as Wilkerson and Boehrer (1992) note, "They can be used to introduce new educational concepts, provoke attitude change, provide practice in solving...problems, and stimulate the desire to acquire new skills" (p. 253).

Cases can be particularly effective in workshops designed to promote specific skills, such as providing effective feedback or using group work (cooperative learning) effectively. I have used two sets of written cases, for instance, in workshops on classroom observations to help faculty learn to provide constructive feedback. In cooperative learning workshops, I and fellow faculty developers have used cases modified to fit the specific circumstances of the adult faculty learners (Millis, 1994). A case entitled, "Bill Jasper's First Night," has been a long-standing mainstay of new faculty orientation at a major adult continuing education institution.

Here are some things—based on adult learning and case study literature—that faculty developers will want to consider when creating and conducting cases with faculty.

Creating or Selecting Case Studies

As this volume attests, many case studies suitable for faculty workshops already exist. It is not necessary to write an original case study unless circumstances, such as specialized audiences or unusual needs, dictate this approach. In creating or selecting a case, faculty developers must keep in mind several key principles. First of all, cases must be authentic, based on actual teaching circumstances. Faculty who may promote theory in their own classrooms become impatient with cases that do not ring true. Cases are often the real experiences of real people with changes to protect identities.

Inviting Faculty Participation

The first principle of adult learning identified by Brookfield (1986) is the importance of voluntary participation. Faculty developers, who deplore the fact that they are often preaching to the choir rather than those sadly in need of teaching enhancement skills, also recognize that mandatory workshops typically breed resentment and hostility.

Thus, the best tactic is to cajole and coerce faculty into workshops that inspire and stimulate them to change

Facilitating Case Discussions

The format must lead to honest, productive exchanges with full participation.

The most commonly used format is the whole-group case method developed by the Harvard Business School (Christensen and Hansen, 1987). This method, used effectively with groups as large as thirty, usually engages all participants in an active, stimulating, teacher-directed discussion. It has the advantage of eliciting multiple viewpoints, drawing on a wide range of experiences. It also results in a shared experience so that all participants are exposed to the same ideas. The facilitators, too, have ample opportunities to offer summaries, redirect misunderstandings, and provide both guidance and a sense of closure.

As a supplement or alternative to the whole-group case method, many trainers have successfully used cooperative learning strategies to train observers, an approach somewhat similar to the problem-centered format described by Wilkerson and Feletti (1989). I have used these case studies with task-oriented groups of four who work together to formulate responses to the focus questions. Group roles—recorder, spokesperson, and leader—can be preassigned or the group members can simply number off, with the understanding that one of them will be called upon to report the group findings, a structure called "Numbered Heads Together" in the cooperative learning literature. In addition to experiencing the power of case studies and acquiring insights into providing effective feedback, participants become familiar with an innovative classroom technique that results in attentiveness, mutual coaching and support, respect for multiple viewpoints, and increased critical thinking.

Using cooperative faculty pairs has also proved to be an effective format. Such pairs approximate more exactly the client-faculty relationship that occurs during a typical consultation process. With pairs, too, virtually everyone is actively engaged—talking and listening reciprocally—in the learning process. The discussion setting provides stimulation but usually offers few risks for the participants, who are coached in behaviors appropriate for their roles. Facilitators, who move congenially among the pairs, often find this format less threatening than the whole-group model because they are not center-stage, responsible for the flow of discussion and any potentially volatile disruptions. Not all facilitators are comfortable thinking on their feet while probing, parrying, challenging, summarizing, and sometimes curtailing the group's comments, skills needed for whole-group discussions.

Not unexpectedly, a great deal of learning and sharing goes on as the participants discuss the case studies in their quads or pairs. Learning also occurs during the report-outs, which can be handled a number of ways. It is important to leave sufficient time for them because faculty, just as students do, like a sense of closure.

Using case studies in workshops is clearly a powerful way to develop or strengthen interpersonal and diagnostic skills. The case studies should be tailored to the participants' needs, goals, and experience level and to the specific institution. Sufficient time must be available to allow them to unfold in all their complexity. The facilitator must select an organizational format which optimizes the time available and the expertise and needs of the participants. Whole-group discussion is often appropriate. I personally prefer placing participants in quads and pairs and using cooperative learning discussion methods for a number of reasons: (1) the large-group format promotes interactions where usually only one individual at a time is "center stage"; in quads or pairs, participants experience not this sequential participation, but simultaneous exchanges actively involving one-fourth to one-half of the workshop participants at any given moment; (2) whole-group formats—particularly if the exchanges are dynamic and thought-provoking—can sometimes provide risky arenas where less vocal members, sometimes women and minorities, are less likely to speak up, as they would in a small group setting; and finally, (3) whole-group exchanges, while intellectually stimulating, may not lead to the skill enhancement—through rehearsal and practice in quads and pairs—that is the whole point of a training session for consultants. Often the best approach will be a combination of the two models, with structured small-group work followed by whole-group discussion for the report-outs so that all experience the same sense of closure. Focus questions need to frame a carefully guided, interactive discussion. These cases, and others like them, give life to an oft-quoted Teton Lakota Native American saying: "Tell me and I'll listen. Show me and I'll understand. Involve me and I'll learn."

---

1. The facts for the two original case studies—and much inspiration—came from William F. Burke, the University of Hawaii at Manoa. Ruth A. Streveler, also of the University of Hawaii, participated too in this collaborative effort.

2. The suggested modifications came from Zoe Irwin, Howard Community College, Maryland.

References:

Brookfield, S. D. (1986). *Understanding and facilitating adult learning: A comprehensive analysis of principles and effective practices.* San Francisco: Jossey-Bass.

Christensen, C. R., and A. J. Hansen (1987). *Teaching and the case method: Text, cases, and readings.* Boston: Harvard Business School.

Millis, B. J. (1994). Conducting cooperative cases. In E.C. Wadsworth (Ed.), *To improve the academy: Resources for faculty, instructional, and organizational development, 13,* 309-328.

Wilkerson, L. and J. Boehrer. (1992). Using cases about teaching for faculty development. In D.H. Wulff and J. D. Nyquist (Eds.), *To improve the academy: Resources for faculty, instructional, and organizational development, 11,* 253-262.

Wilkerson, L. and G. Feletti. (1989). Problem-based learning: One
    approach to increasing student participation. In A.F. Lucas (Ed.),
    The department chairperson's role in enhancing college teaching
    (pp. 51-60), New directions for teaching and learning, no. 37. San
    Francisco: Jossey-Bass.

Wlodkowski, R. J. (1993). *Enhancing adult motivation to learn: A guide to*
    improving instruction and increasing learner achievement. San
    Francisco: Jossey-Bass.

Appendix

The Case Method's Nine Rules of Engagement (ROE)

1. PREPARE THOROUGHLY. Read the case, reflect on its
content, and discuss it with others before coming to class.

2. TAKE *"Freefall"* RISKS. Express your views without
prejudging them. We want to hear what you have to say
because you may have that golden angle or perspective
that helps us to break through confusion and ignorance.

3. LISTEN CAREFULLY. Focus on the other person's
thoughts, not his/her efforts to express them. Ask questions to clarify what is said. Restate the person's remarks
to be sure you understand his/her point.

4. PROMOTE DEMOCRACY. Become suspicious when-
ever everyone agrees that a judgment is true or that an
argument is successful. Encourage a wide variety of
viewpoints and opinions. Avoid "group think," peer
pressure, and the convergence of opinion. (The more
views that you entertain, the more likely it is that you will
discover the internal logic of the situation you are assess-
ing and find the best available course of action.)

5. EXTEND CHARITY. *Always* give your colleagues the
benefit of the doubt.

6. PRACTICE CIVILITY. *Never forget* that your colleagues have a fundamental, inviolable worth as human beings and always must be respected as such. Avoid dealing in personalities or making personal attacks. Leave your ego in a box in your room. The case discussion classroom is a forum and a laboratory—not an arena. We are here to hammer out new levels of understanding, new agendas for investigation, and tentative solutions—we are not here to hammer on each other. Encourage others to take part and applaud the efforts of those who do.

7. EMBRACE AMBIGUITY. There is very little "closure" in life—learn to live with it. Most of the "solutions" we discover are at best tentative and hypothetical. What we must do is use the best available means to reach the best working hypotheses—and that means drawing upon the strengths of the Learning Community.

8. BUILD COMMUNITY. Faithfully observe the ROE and gently remind others that they should do the same. Constantly seek new ways to perpetuate and expand the community.

9. TAKE RESPONSIBILITY. Someone once said that the 10 most important words in life are, "If it is to be, it is up to me." Believe it.

(Prepared by Major "Pat" Tower for courses at the United States Air Force Academy.)

Using Cases to Create a Culture of Teaching and Learning

Pat Hutchings

A number of years ago at AAHE's National Conference, K. Patricia Cross called on audience members to "take teaching seriously." Today on campuses across the country efforts are underway to do just that.

New approaches to teaching and learning are capturing the attention of growing numbers of faculty. Strategies for collaborative and cooperative learning are changing the way students and faculty interact in the classroom; the assessment movement and the practice of classroom research are helping faculty ask important questions about who their students are and how they learn best. Service learning and experiential learning are on the rise, as are problem-, project-, and case-based approaches.

But beyond new strategies and methods, there's a growing recognition that what's also needed is a campus culture in which good practice can thrive, one where faculty talk together about teaching, inquire into its effects, and take collective responsibility for its quality. *Cases* can be a powerful route to developing such a culture.

Cases are not new, of course. They have a long-established place in law and business, where they are both carriers of the "stuff" of the field and vehicles for teaching it. In social work and psychology, cases and case study are a recognized form of research and professional inquiry. In teacher education, work is now underway to develop and use cases as curricular materials, and several volumes of such cases are now available. But with a few exceptions (most notably the work of Roland Christensen at Harvard University) the potential of cases for improving college teaching has only recently begun to garner campus attention.

My own foray into the use of cases as vehicles for prompting more and better discussion about teaching began in the summer of 1990, with funding from the Lilly Endowment Inc.; AAHE launched a three-year project to begin answering those questions. Our aim was to develop cases about college teaching and learning in a variety of disciplines—materials that could be used to open up the traditionally private world of the classroom to collaborative, reflective discussion among faculty. In the subsequent years, we have developed a clearinghouse of cases, run scores of workshops on case writing and discussion, and established a summer "working conference" on cases as tools for reflective teaching and learning.

But most important, as evidenced by this volume, we have found good colleagues who have embraced the idea of cases and adapted it to their own contexts and needs.

Defining the "genre"

As illustrated by the cases in this volume, there is no standard formula for cases. Some are longer, some shorter; some in the first person, some in third. Some focus mostly on the teacher's experience, some are told from the student's point of view and evoke important discussion of learning as well as teaching. Nevertheless, in the midst of this variety, there's a core conception of the "genre," and it's possible to point to four features shared by cases likely to prompt more reflective teaching.

A first feature is *authenticity.* Cases prompt serious discussion and reflection when, and only when, faculty find them believable, lifelike, realistic. This is not to say that cases must be literal accounts of actual incidents, though they may be; it *is* to say that the characters, situations, and dilemmas entailed must ring true for faculty readers, who will be quick, says veteran case writer William Welty, to "smell contrivance." Seen from the point of view of the case writer, the issue is not "real vs. fiction" but how to select and represent experience so as to prompt meaningful discussion of teaching and learning.

Concrete detail is a second feature of cases that work. Concreteness helps create authenticity, but its importance also lies in the fact that teaching does not occur in a vacuum. As Kenneth Eble noted, "it is attention to the particulars that brings any craft of art to a high degree of development" (*The Craft of Teaching*, p. 6). So too with teaching—and it's the capacity of cases to represent the particulars of who's teaching what, to whom, under what conditions, that makes them powerful in raising pedagogical issues.

For most readers, the power of cases lies in large part in a third feature, their *narrative form*. This is not to say that cases must read like short stories; one of the examples in the AAHE case clearinghouse (and published in a 1993 AAHE publication) is organized more around data about students than around a central protagonist with whom we identify. Nevertheless, cases engage our attention for some of the same reasons a piece of fiction does: we read to watch the action unfold, to find out what happens next, often identifying with the actors, feeling personally involved in their choices, playing out the consequences....

Finally, cases work because they're *open-ended*. Longtime Harvard case writer Abby J. Hansen speaks of cases as having an "irreducible core of ambiguity" (Christensen, p. 56). Complex and information-rich, cases depict teaching and learning incidents that are deliberately open to interpretation—raising questions rather than answering them, encouraging problem solving, calling forth collective faculty intelligence and varied perspectives, promoting more reflective practice.

A Look at Current Practice

Over the past five years, scores of campuses and hundreds of faculty have discovered the power of cases to prompt good talk about good teaching—and learning. Even more, faculty and faculty groups have found ways to tailor cases to their own local needs.

At Eastern Michigan University, faculty in a number of departments began using cases to solve problems they faced with their own students. In the math department, for instance, student under preparation has been a persistent issue, the subject of ongoing hallway conversation. But most of that conversation, department members told me during a campus visit, has been "unproductive moaning and groaning." Seeing cases as a way to focus the conversation and move it to a more productive level, math faculty have begun writing cases about their own classes to discuss with colleagues at Friday afternoon department meetings. Programming offered through the Faculty Center for Instructional Excellence, directed by Deborah DeZure, now regularly includes sessions dedicated to the discussion and writing of cases; the point is not to produce highly polished products but to get enough of the story "on the table" so that EMU faculty can problem solve together.

In the state of Washington, cases are being used not only to explore an issue but to advance an important educational idea. Through the Washington Center for Improving the Quality of Undergraduate Education, an interinstitutional consortium founded at Evergreen State College, a faculty group developed a set of cases focused on their work in collaborative "learning communities." Cases, they have found, provide an appropriately interactive way to invite other faculty (students and administrators, too) to participate in and advance collaborative teaching and learning.

Like faculty in the Washington Center case group, faculty at Florida Community College at Jacksonville have found that cases are powerful not only in their finished form but as they're being developed. Several years ago an interdisciplinary group of FCCJ faculty began meeting to write cases about issues in their own classrooms; what they found was that the process of crafting their own experiences into a meaningful narrative was itself reflection-prompting, and a wonderful occasion for good conversation about teaching and learning.

New teachers and graduate teaching assistants are, predictably, an audience for cases in many settings. They were, for instance, the intended audience for a set of cases about the teaching of writing developed under the auspices of the Alliance for Undergraduate Education, a consortium of sixteen public research universities. But in workshop settings where the cases have been discussed, their power to engage faculty at *all* levels of experience has quickly become clear. The idea, as one of the five faculty authors explained to me, is to pose common problems in the teaching of writing in a way that will help people solve them in their own context.

The above is of course a sampling, not an exhaustive list, of current uses of cases for "faculty development." Now, with the appearance of this volume, a new piece is added to the picture: cases aimed explicitly at issues of adult education.

The Power of Cases

One reason is that cases have "caught on" as tools for reflective discussion and improvement of teaching is that *good cases are just plain interesting:* they tell a story, involving us with particular people in particular settings whose problems we puzzle over, debate about, "relate to." Not everyone is as enthusiastic as the faculty member in an AAHE case workshop who explained, "This is the best discussion of teaching I've had in twenty years." But even skeptics of "faculty development" find it hard not to get caught up in the discussion of teaching and learning when cases are the prompt. For many, a lively, concrete discussion of a case is a welcome alternative to the workshop in which some expert on education delivers up yet another disembodied teaching technique.

A second reason is that *cases put permission in the air* for faculty to talk openly about their teaching. They provide an occasion for faculty to share experiences and expertise—and this at the time when many faculty have twenty-plus years in the classroom to draw on. "Cases have helped us realize the expertise that faculty on this campus have," says one of the faculty from Florida Community College at Jacksonville who has been active in using cases there. But cases also make it possible for faculty to reveal uncertainties, frustration, and failure. Permission to do so comes, as one faculty member working with AAHE noted, because case discussion is "non ego-invested." The conversation starts not with *my* teaching but with *someone else's;* the invitation is out to think aloud and try out new ideas in what Pace University case writers and teachers Bill Welty and Rita Silverman describe as the "learning laboratory" provided by a good case. The risk is low, the benefits high.

A fourth reason to try cases is that faculty involved in a case discussion about teaching are, along the way, learning *a method they can try out* in their own classrooms. The pedagogy of the case method is active learning at its best, and many faculty who have attended workshops on cases about teaching and learning have been quick to see the potential for cases in their own classroom, used to teach key concepts in more lively, active ways. Indeed, some would argue that it's in the classroom that cases and the case method of discussion will do their most important work when it comes to the improvement of teaching.

Fifth, *cases create a sense of community* where, for most teachers, isolation has ruled the day. Following a case discussion I facilitated among some 100 colleagues from the Vermont State Colleges, one participant wrote me a note saying "It was wonderful to hear how thoughtful and caring my colleagues are about teaching." Faculty participating in the Washington Center project on cases report a similar satisfaction ("You may leave the session not only more impressed by your colleagues but liking them more as well.") and also note how, in well-run discussions, "the community intelligence evolves" (Washington, pp. 4-5). Such comments bring to mind current concerns about the reward system for teaching, reminding us that promotion, tenure, and merit pay are not the only coin in the realm. The experience of being part of something bigger that matters, the feeling of colleagueship, the sense of collective responsibility and efficacy...these too are rewards that faculty value and that cases can deliver.

Finally, *cases make sense because they fill a gap.* There's an exciting array of new (or newly interesting) methods and approaches faculty today are experimenting with in their own classrooms: classroom research, collaborative and co-operative learning, experiential learning, service learning....The number of conferences and publications for learning about such strategies seems ever on the rise. But while new techniques are important, something larger may be needed more: habits of inquiry into teaching and learning, regular occasions for informed conversation about it, and a sense of collective responsibility for the education students receive. What's needed, in short, and what cases can help create, is a change in attitudes toward teaching.

Cases and a View of Teaching

Cases have a special power to get people talking with each other about teaching—trying out ideas, trading points of view, sharing stories, being energized, and (not incidentally) having fun doing it. Such outcomes are, I suspect, sufficient reason for trying cases on many campuses, where the level of conversation about teaching is low to nonexistent. But there's a deeper rationale for cases, as well, one that begins not with the fact of good discussion but with cases themselves as a genre particularly well matched to emerging conceptions of effective teaching.

Traditionally, on most campuses and for many faculty, teaching has been "constructed" primarily in terms of *technique* or *method.* There's truth to this view; certainly technique and method play a role in good teaching. But what a technique-oriented view of teaching leaves out of the picture is the scholarly, intellectual *substance* of teaching, an omission that serves to feed the view that research is serious, real work, deserving of collegial attention, and teaching is...well, a task to be done, a "load," a purely private and mostly technical activity.

Recently, work by people like Ernest Boyer and Lee Shulman has put forward a different, more scholarly view of teaching. In *Scholarship Reconsidered* Boyer argues that we need a broader conception of scholarship, one that encompasses not only research (the scholarship of discovery) but other kinds of intellectual work that faculty do, including teaching (1990). Shulman has argued that excellent teachers have what he calls "pedagogical content knowledge"— not just method, and not just subject matter expertise, but a repertoire for transforming what they know for students.

In short, attention to teaching methods is necessary but not sufficient—not if we want deeper, longer-lasting improvement. What's needed for improvement is a new, scholarly view of teaching that lends itself to serious, collegial discussion and reflection.

Cases have, in this sense, a special power to improve teaching—not so much by suggesting what to do in situation x, or how to do this or that on Monday morning (though certainly one may learn strategies and methods from cases). The distinctive contribution of cases is in promoting *a way of thinking about teaching* as a complex, intellectually engaging process of making decisions and solving problems in ambiguous situations. To put it differently, the use of cases is predicated on a view—like Shulman's—that the knowledge effective teachers bring to their work (or need to be able to bring) is not simply a knowledge of methods but of substance and ideas—about one's field, about students, about learning...and about the complex relationships among these "variables" in real classrooms.

In sum, cases give teaching its due as an intellectual activity...and teachers a vehicle for intellectual community.

References:

Boyer, E.L. (1990). *Scholarship reconsidered: Priorities of the professoriate.*
    Princeton, N.J.: Carnegie Foundation for the Advancement of
    Teaching.

Christensen, C. R., with A. J. Hansen. (1987). *Teaching and the case
    method.* Boston, MA: Harvard Business School.

Eble, K. (1988). *The craft of teaching* (2nd ed.). San Francisco: Jossey-
    Bass.

Shulman, L. S. (1989). Toward a Pedagogy of Substance. *AAHE Bulletin
    41* (10): 8-13.

Washington Center for Improving the Quality of Undergraduate
    Education. (1993). *The washington center casebook on collaborative
    teaching and learning.* Olympia, WA: The Washington Center.

Author's Note:
This essay is adapted from material that originally appeared in my
monograph *Using Cases to Improve College Teaching: A Guide to More
Reflective Practice*, published in 1993 by the American Association for
Higher Education, Washington, DC.

Including Adult Students in Case Discussions

Louise Love

It is through dialogue that we attempt to understand—to learn—what is valid in the assertions made by others and attempt to achieve consensual validation for our own assertions. Consequently, education for adults may be understood as centrally involved in creating and facilitating dialogic communities to enable learners to engage in rational discourse and action. (Mezirow, p. 354)

One of the successful "dialogic communities" that has been established outside of the classroom for the adult learners of Northwestern's University College is the forum in which students and faculty discuss together issues of pedagogy, classroom management, and faculty/student relationships that are raised in published "cases." As Mezirow suggests, the bringing together of individuals with different perspectives to engage in dialogue on issues of mutual concern has enabled all of the participants—faculty, students, and administrators—to challenge assumptions, evaluate assertions, and arrive at new ways of understanding the things that transpire in our classrooms.

These discussions, initially based on cases published by the Harvard Business School, were organized as a faculty-only component of a varied menu of offerings sponsored by the University College Faculty Development Program. Within two years, however, the first joint faculty/student case discussion was piloted. The impetus for this experiment came from members of the Student Advisory Board. They were seeking a forum in which to engage faculty in dialogue on a variety of issues ranging from the selection of textbooks and specific course offerings to the rights and responsibilities of students and student expectations of faculty. It occurred to the deans of University College and to the Coordinator of the Faculty Development Program that a ready-made forum existed in the form of the case discussions. Although the students may have made their request with specific grievances and personal issues in mind, we believed that the likelihood of constructive and productive dialogue would be enhanced by displacing the discussion from the specific concerns of individuals and raising issues through hypothetical cases.

The first joint faculty/student case discussion was scheduled for January 30, 1993. The dialogue that ensued was enlightening for all concerned. One of the early revelations of these joint case discussions was that the premise that there was a distinct "student perspective," different from and perhaps at odds with an imagined "faculty perspective," was simply wrong. Many of the participants entered into the joint sessions with the assumption that faculty would typically advocate on the side of strict limits, absolute standards, and clear-cut consequences in discussing the particulars of a given case, and that students would generally advocate for flexible limits, relative standards, and negotiable consequences. That assumption was quickly proven false. It has become clear that students are often less conflicted about enforcing strict standards of performance and about imposing the consequences of failure to meet these standards than are faculty. Simply put, students can be tough on themselves. This has been just one of the surprising—and enlightening—results of including students in the discussions and actually hearing their points of view.

As a result of the success of the first session and several subsequent joint sessions, two combined case discussions have become an integral part of the annual schedule of the Faculty Development Program. We want to ensure that students and faculty may regularly participate in this type of "dialogic community" and have an opportunity to evaluate their views in the light of a variety of perspectives. We have become convinced that the benefits of these joint sessions accrue not only to the students, but to the faculty and the administrators who participate as well.

The frank sharing of opinions in response to a hypothetical case has led to a deeper, more informed understanding of the needs and attitudes of each group. Because the students and faculty are all adults and of widely varying ages, issues of authority are not drawn along seniority lines. Furthermore, it is not always apparent which participants are students and which are faculty, and this anonymity promotes candor in the expression of views.

> In *The Skillful Teacher*, Stephen D. Brookfield emphasizes trust as the basis for learning. Trust between teachers and students is the affective glue binding educational relationships together.... The more profound and meaningful the learning is to students, the more they need to be able to trust their teachers. (Brookfield, p. 163)

Engaging in case discussions with members of the faculty promotes the trust that Brookfield finds so essential. He identifies the two components of trust as "credibility" and "authenticity." In the case discussions, students see the genuine struggles and dilemmas, the concerns and commitment that are part of the faculty's lives as educators. Even for those students who do not actually attend the sessions, simply knowing that the opportunity is available enhances the atmosphere of trust and collegiality that we wish to foster throughout the "culture" of University College. In this setting, students, faculty, and administrators come together and share their bewilderment and their frustrations as well as their creativity, commitment, and problem-solving abilities. With the power gradient neutralized, all of the participants are equal in authority and the opportunity for mutual trust is maximized.

If further support is needed for the inclusion of students in case discussions, I would submit this book as evidence of its value. The original idea for bringing together a set of cases based on the experience of faculty, students, and administrators in an evening adult program came from a student participating in one of our joint case discussions. At this session on January 29, 1994, a student (an undergraduate in her forties) who had attended earlier sessions pointed out that the Harvard cases typically describe situations with traditional-age graduate students who attend business school full-time. In the case under discussion on that particular day, one of the factors in the conflict was the student's financial dependence on her parents. The University College student pointed out that it was difficult for her to relate to the situation because she had been self-supporting for many years; indeed, she had dependent children of her own—one of them in college. This observation and follow-up conversations have resulted in this volume. The cases have been written by faculty, administrators, and students; and we anticipate that representatives from each of these groups will participate in the discussions. Conceived in this way, the book may accomplish one of Mezirow's stated desiderata:

> . . .assisting those who are fulfilling adult roles to understand the meaning of their experience by participating more fully and freely in rational discourse to validate expressed ideas and to take action upon the resulting insights. (*Idem.*)

A variety of actions have resulted from the discussions that have taken place in these forums. Syllabi have been redesigned; new textbooks have been adopted. Most visibly, this book has been published. The book stands, then, not only as the embodiment of a student's vision of an appropriate resource for use in a dialogic community of adults, it is also "living" testimony to the quality of ideas that can result when students are included as equal stakeholders in the process of discussing cases.

References:

Brookfield, S. D. (1990). *The skillful teacher*. San Francisco: Jossey-Bass.
Mezirow, J. and Associates. (1990). *Fostering critical   reflection in adulthood*. San Francisco: Jossey-Bass.

Part II:
Cases from a Faculty Perspective

Of Pride and Prejudice
Louise Love

Luther Andrews had taught classes in literature and English composition at Wilson University for almost twenty-five years. Approaching fifty, he still had boyish good looks and the ebullient energy that had made him a popular teacher with men and women alike. Students were stimulated by Luther's genuine passion for literature, his humor, his startling insights, and his gift for showing connections between popular culture and the "canon." Still an eligible bachelor in spite of several long-term relationships—some with former students—Luther was a little prone to show off, perhaps; but his showmanship played well with his students most of the time. Luther's flair for the outrageous kept the classroom lively, and the students appreciated this—especially after a long day at work.

This fall, Luther was scheduled to teach Twentieth Century American Literature—a course he had taught a dozen or more times—for adult students in the evening program. The English Department gave him a free hand in constructing his syllabus. And now, as the century was in its final years, he was struck by the extent to which his choice of readings had changed over the years. How different twentieth century American literature looked even in the span of his own teaching career. On the first night of class, after handing out the syllabus, he decided to give the class some historical perspective on this point.

"When I chose the readings for this class," he began, "I was reminded of those bomber crews in the World War II movies. You know, they always had a white guy, a black guy, and a Jewish guy. Today, of course, the third guy would be Hispanic and one of them would be gay." Subdued, but appreciative, laughter came from the class. "Of course, there would not be a woman on a bomber crew. Everyone knew that women could not be trusted with something as valuable as an airplane with bombs in it. The idea of 'woman' was just implicit in the men's desire to win the war and go home." The students were giving Luther their full attention, so he instinctively continued, digressing more than he had originally intended.

"The 1990s version of inclusiveness is a little different, of course. It looks more like the movie *To Wong Foo, Thanks for Everything, Julie Newmar*." There were some blank faces among the students; so, Luther asked. "Has anyone seen it? It's on video." Five or so of the twenty-two students raised their hands and nodded to show that they were following his point. Luther elucidated, "Three drag queens take a road trip. One is high-WASP, one is ultra-Soul, and one is Latino. Obviously, all of them are gay. There are still no women in the 'bomber crew'; but, now, all the guys are girls—sort of. Things have gotten a lot more complicated, ambiguous, and ironic. Think about what that says about Hollywood's view of the American viewing public. . .our sophistication, our acceptance level, our sense of what is and what is not sacred." Luther decided just to leave that point for the students to ponder and get back to the business of the class. But first, he muttered to himself, barely audibly, "Still the media expect us to be up-in-arms every time the President unzips." This was not meant for the class, but students in the front seats heard him.

Using his full, professorial voice, Luther continued, "So, what does all of this have to do with your syllabus? Well, up to the sixties, a class like this would have been all Hemingway, Fitzgerald, and Faulkner. Playwrights were O'Neill, Miller, Tennessee Williams. Poets? Frost, e.e. cummings, maybe Sandburg out here in the Midwest. All white guys. You could never get away with that today." Luther paused to let his point sink in. Then, he went on, "Just look at who wins the Nobel prize for literature. Which American gets it in 1954? Ernest Hemingway. What happens in 1993? Toni Morrison. It's all politics, ladies and gentlemen. Politics and fashion." By now, Luther was waving the syllabus in front of the class. Some students were clearly entertained by his disquisition; others looked puzzled.

The weeks went by with students dipping into a rich sampler of American literature from Emily Dickinson, William Faulkner, and Ralph Ellison to Rita Dove, Truman Capote, and Scott Momaday. In addition to class discussion and entries in personal journals, students were asked to write three five-page "reaction papers" on works by authors covered in the course or, with Luther's approval, works by other American authors. At least one of the works chosen had to be pre-WWII. Each student would choose one of these papers as the basis for a final ten-to-twelve page critique. Luther said he would schedule individual conferences with each student to discuss his or her proposal for the final paper. He held these conferences at Rozinante Cafe, a local coffee shop, that was known among English majors as "The LOO" (Luther's Other Office).

* * * * *

Darcy Herbst was a writing major in Luther's class. On the first night of Twentieth Century American Literature, she introduced herself as a financial planner and said that, after receiving her undergraduate degree, she was planning to work on an MFA and eventually teach writing and establish a literary journal. What she did not tell the class was that she had completed two years of college at an Ivy League school fifteen years earlier and had dropped out because of her family's money problems. She went to work full-time at twenty and helped get her parents back on their feet. Now that she had the resources—this time her own money—she had returned to school part-time in the evening to complete the degree she had started what seemed like a long time ago. Financially successful, Darcy had put her literary aspirations on hold and, deep down, felt that she had been deprived of a reasonable chance to fulfill her destiny—as a writer. Darcy had heard good things about Luther's classes, but she was not favorably impressed on the first night of class. His bravado reminded her of the men with whom she worked in investments. "Self-infatuated," she thought. "Thinks he's God's gift." Nevertheless, she believed he could run a good class, and she was eager to learn more about American literature. For the first of the reaction papers, Darcy asked Luther if she could depart from the syllabus and write on Pearl Buck's *The Good Earth*. She noticed, when she asked Luther this question, a little wince pass across his face. Luther hesitated before answering, visibly struggling to frame his words tactfully.

"Actually, Darcy," he spoke slowly and deliberately, "I would prefer that you choose someone else." He thought again for a while before resuming. "Mainly because I haven't read Pearl Buck myself, and I'm afraid I wouldn't be able to do justice to your reaction paper." Luther hesitated; then continued, "Um, also, her work is not considered to be of the same. . .well. . .complexity as the other authors we've been reading. I think we'll both be more satisfied with another author."

Darcy was both surprised and offended. She had revered Pearl Buck since childhood. Her mother and her grandmother had often said, when Darcy wrote stories for school, that she might be another Pearl Buck when she grew up. Perhaps, she thought, the teacher had misunderstood her. "Isn't Pearl Buck a significant 20th-century American author? She won the Nobel prize for literature back in the days when you said it was all white males. I can't believe you have a Ph.D. and you haven't read her books."

Luther could see that he was on sensitive ground but was not inclined to yield. He was the teacher, after all; and it was a "received" opinion among his acquaintance that Buck's work was mediocre. Her name was invoked among the literati to signify "overrated." He remembered reading back in the 1960s the reaction of the London Times to Steinbeck's receiving the Nobel Prize. The Times questioned the standards by which the award was given when it recognized authors such as Steinbeck and Pearl Buck. It had not occurred to Luther that people still read her work. His opinion may have been more obvious than he realized when he reiterated his advice to Darcy that she find someone on the syllabus to write about. He thought no more about it until the papers were handed in.

After reading a number of student papers on works by Nathaniel West, Lillian Hellman, Carson McCullers, Luther came to Darcy's paper—written on *The Good Earth* by Pearl S. Buck. Offended by her blatant defiance of his authority, Luther contemplated giving the paper back without comment, without a grade, and without credit. But, partly out of curiosity and partly out of the will to be reasonable, Luther relented and read the paper. Not having read the book, he could not evaluate the analysis; however, the writing was competent and mature. He decided to accept the paper and give it a C. He wrote in his comments that the writing had earned a B but that he had lowered the grade one point for not answering the assignment.

* * * * *

The phone rang in the office of Julia Brachman, Darcy Herbst's academic adviser. When the voicemail clicked on, Darcy left a message saying that she had to arrange a time to meet. She said that one of her teachers was a sexist and a racist. She said it was urgent that the school know what goes on in his class. When Julia heard the message, she let out a little groan. Darcy was a "high maintenance" advisee who had complained about a number of teachers in the past and had even taken her complaints to the Provost's office when she did not get the response she wanted. A talented, almost-straight-A student, Darcy was, in Julia's view, a rigid perfectionist with a tendency to be literal and legalistic. Julia had observed that Darcy's complaints in the past, while ostensibly about teaching methods and school policy, always got around eventually to grading standards and, specifically, the grades on her assignments. Julia had also observed that all of Darcy's complaints, with one exception, had been directed at men. Reflexively, Julia looked up on the computer to see which classes Darcy was in. When she saw Luther Andrews's twentieth-century American literature class, she guessed that his was probably the course in question. She knew of Luther's flamboyance and his history of romantic entanglements. She also knew that he was an inspiring teacher for most students and a great friend to the evening school. She hated to think that he had incurred the well-known wrath of Darcy Herbst.

At the meeting with Julia, Darcy said that she was appalled that a school with a fine reputation like Wilson University would employ a teacher who believed that women were inferior to men and who thinks that only white men deserve to receive the Nobel Prize for literature. She told Julia that Luther had made it clear on the first night of class that Toni Morrison received the Nobel Prize only because of "politics and fashion" and he later told her that Pearl Buck's work was inferior—even though he admitted that he hadn't read it. She said that Luther gave her an undeservedly low grade on her reaction paper because she wrote about an author he held in contempt—even though the Nobel Prize committee recognized her as the best living author in the world in 1938. Darcy went on, "He even said that everyone knows that women cannot be trusted to pilot a plane. How can you let him evaluate the work of female students?"

The upshot of Darcy's meeting with Julia was a request to have the chair of the English department re-evaluate her paper. Darcy also told Julia that she refused to meet the teacher off campus "over drinks" to discuss her final paper. Julia listened to Darcy's allegations, told her that the teacher had been on Wilson's faculty for many years and had an excellent reputation, and assured her that she would ask the chair of the English department to speak with Professor Andrews about the comments he had made in class. She told Darcy that the time for challenging grades would come at the end of the semester and advised her to keep all papers, comments, and the course syllabus in case she decided to make such an appeal when the time came. (Julia could see that, in fact, Darcy had already documented Luther's behavior in great detail and could cite precise dates and times for his "misdeeds.") Julia told Darcy to continue going to class and that she would be back in touch after she had spoken to the chair of the English department.

* * * * *

It took several days for Julia to reach the chair of the English department. By that time, Darcy had gone to the Women's Center and registered a formal charge against Luther Andrews. She did not inform Julia of this move because she felt that her adviser had not been sufficiently alarmed by the report Darcy gave her of Luther Andrews's behavior. Without any warning, therefore, Luther was summoned in writing to appear before a hearing board to answer the charges that had been leveled against him. The charges, which were detailed in the summons, presented a picture of Luther that was completely foreign to his image of himself: gender bias. . .sexual harrassment. . .racism. . . unprofessional behavior. Who were they talking about? Luther wondered if he should call a lawyer.

* * * * *

Questions:
1. Is there evidence of any real bias on the part of Luther Andrews?
2. What missteps, if any, did Luther Andrews make that left him open to misinterpretation?
3. What allowances might be made for a successful teacher's idiosyncratic style?
4. Could Julia Brachman, the adviser, have done more to head off this situation?

Stuart

Joan and Gary Phillips

After the third week of the semester in his modern European history course, the professor was packing up his material and preparing to head for home. It was a few minutes after nine in the evening—this was an evening adult education class—and he was thinking about the hour-and-a-half drive that faced him.

"Excuse me, um, Dr. Tyler," a voice said.

Dr. Tyler looked up to see Stuart. Dr. Tyler guessed that Stuart was perhaps thirty-one years old. He wore blue jeans and a university sweatshirt. During these first few weeks in class he had spoken up occasionally during class discussions, but Dr. Tyler noted that many of his comments seemed to stray from the point of the readings and ideas they were discussing. He recalled that Stuart said in the introductions the first evening that he had been pursuing his degree part time for several years and that he took two—or was it three?—classes per semester.

"Yes?" Dr. Tyler answered cautiously.

"I just wanted to let you know," Stuart said, with what seemed a casual tone of voice, "that I have a learning disability." He said that this disability had been only recently identified at the university health center. He went on to say that, because of the disability, "I'll need some extra time to complete the reading assignments in your class."

Dr. Tyler was curious about the nature of the disability, but his curiosity was more than matched by his fatigue after a long day. His mind still on the long drive home, he agreed quickly and wished Stuart a good night. He did not think about Stuart or his statement at all in the following week.

In the next class period, during the discussion about the reading, Dr. Tyler noted that Stuart was uncharacteristically silent. He asked him a question about the reading, and Stuart stared at him blankly for a moment, then said, "I'm not finished with the reading yet. Don't you remember? Our conversation?"

Somewhat abashed, Dr. Tyler said, "Yes, yes," and went on to another topic. At the end of class, as Stuart was leaving, Dr. Tyler motioned him over and asked the specific nature of the learning disability.

Stuart fidgeted with his books and said, "Oh, I don't know. I just need more time to do things like reading, more time than most people." He flushed briefly, and Dr. Tyler, not wanting to embarrass him about such a sensitive thing, did not pursue the matter.

The week before the midterm exam, Stuart approached Dr. Tyler again after class. With no preliminaries, Stuart said, "I need to take my exam in a room by myself where I won't be distracted by anyone. It's my learning disability. Distraction is a problem for me." His tone was more assertive than it had been in their previous conversations.

Dr. Tyler thought he had heard it all in his 12 years of teaching adult education courses, but this was a new request for him. "Well," he said, "I don't know. I don't know where we would do it. I suppose someone would have to be there to proctor the exam." He paused, then proceeded gingerly: "Stuart, just what is your learning disability? I mean, what is the specific diagnosis?"

"I can't remember the specific name. You know, all that doctor talk sounds like gibberish. 'Post- something,' or 'anti-something.'"

Suddenly, Dr. Tyler made a decision. "Well, I'm afraid I couldn't grant a request such as this one without some kind of documentation. A report from a doctor."

"You mean like proof? You mean you don't trust me?"

"I just mean it will be better for both of us if I know the exact nature of the disability. I will be able to better help you with this course." As Dr. Tyler said this, he realized that in fact he did not trust him.

"Well I can't get the report by next week. Call Dean

Goodwin. He'll tell you all about it. I've talked to him about it a lot."

Dr. Tyler said that he would call the dean and that if he confirmed the situation, he would make arrangements for Stuart to take his exam away from distractions.

Dean Goodwin did confirm that Stuart had a learning disability, that it was documented, and that it required him to avoid distraction in high-stress situations such as an exam. He did not, however, know of any other special consider-ations that would be necessary. Dean Goodwin suggested that Stuart could take the exam in the glass-enclosed confer-ence room next to the staff offices. That way, Dr. Tyler, or a proctor, could monitor him from time to time.

The night of the exam, both Stuart and Dr. Tyler arrived early for class. When Dr. Tyler showed Stuart the room in which he would take the exam, Stuart was visibly upset. "I can't take the exam in that room. I've taken exams in there before. It's too noisy with the staff working right outside."

Dr. Tyler thought of saying that the staff would be leav-ing in just a half hour, but didn't feel like getting into an argument. He and Stuart walked through the halls looking for empty rooms. Stuart rejected the first two as either "too small" or "too stuffy." Finally he acceded to the third one, rested his bag on a chair, and sat in another chair. Dr. Tyler gave him the exam, glancing at his watch and noticing he was already ten minutes late for his other students.

"I can't do this," Stuart exclaimed.

"Can't do what?"

"I can't do an essay test! It's my learning disability. Last semester, my professor gave me a special multiple-choice test because of my problem."

"Stuart," Dr. Tyler said, "I truly want to help. But you mentioned nothing about test format, and you still have not told me exactly what your disability entails or given me any documentation." He glanced at his watch again and, as Stuart started to speak, held up his palms. "Okay, okay. Just do the best you can on the exam. We'll see how you do and talk again next week. I'll be up to check on you every so often."

"To check on me? But I can't have any distractions! Dr. Tyler, my whole life I have felt so...so slow, so left behind. Now, finally, I know the reason. It's not my fault, like I always thought it was. It's this learning disability. It's like... it's like not being able to walk. If I couldn't walk, you wouldn't expect me to take an exam on the third story of a building without an elevator, would you? You seem to be set on making me fail in this course. It's not fair."

Dr. Tyler repeated that Stuart should take the test and "see what happened." Edging toward the door, he said, "I have to get down to the other students. We'll talk later."

Dr. Tyler gave Stuart a C on his exam—which, he admitted to himself, was probably slightly higher than the grade he deserved. Nevertheless, Stuart was devastated by the grade, and the semester went downhill from there. Dr. Tyler refused to give him a makeup exam, but did offer to put Stuart in touch with a tutor, an offer which Stuart did not pursue. Stuart became more sullen and fell further behind as the semester went on. Any discussions Stuart and Dr. Tyler had ended up in a wrangle over procedures. The funny thing was, Dr. Tyler felt deep down that Stuart had potential as a student, and he accepted his comparison between someone who had a physical disability and someone who had a learning disability. He himself had a cousin with a serious developmental disability, and in an unexamined sort of way he believed that the "system" had an obligation to be flexible and provide opportunities for such people. Yet with Stuart he made no headway. By the next-to-last week of the semester, Dr. Tyler found himself thinking, "What the heck. He'll get a C, which certainly isn't failing, and this nightmare will be over."

Questions:

1. What could Dr. Tyler have done differently to avoid these

problems with Stuart? Should he have been stricter? Been more lenient?

2. Should Dr. Tyler have been more insistent about seeing documentation of the disability? Would such insistence have been an invasion of Stuart's privacy?

3. How could Dean Goodwin have assisted in this difficulty?

4. Discuss Stuart's responsibilities in this case. How could Dr. Tyler have helped Stuart fulfill those responsibilities?

5. What special requests have you encountered from adult students that you have been hesitant to grant? What special requests have you been willing to grant?

6. How do you define expectations in class up front to help preclude inappropriate special requests? How do you do so without setting an unnecessarily rigid tone for the semester?

Practicing Theory
Mary Hanson Harrison

In *Epistle VII*, Plato concludes that knowledge is acquired after long study and with the aid of a teacher not as an authority, but as a guide, and as one who is also learning. I have always liked the idea of teaching as a sort of communal search. Plato, however, has his itinerary carefully mapped out. Today, the route seems less certain.

Last semester, I taught a course on contemporary literary theory, a field more often filled with detours than direct routes, to a class of adults in the continuing education division of a large university. It was the first time I had taught the course, and, I believe, the first time it had been offered in the division. My goal was to explore various theories of criticism and come to grips with some of the underlying philosophical issues. We would pursue these goals by focusing on the metaphor of women as it appeared in works by authors including Heidegger, Irigarary, and Flaubert.

Literary criticism involves many sensitive and often precarious topics, such as politics, multiculturalism, feminism, and deconstruction. So I was prepared for the inevitable moans and groans during the introduction of these difficult texts, as well as issues dealing with "political correctness." However, I was not quite prepared for what occurred on the first night of class.

Session I: The session began in the midst of a blizzard, and I remarked to the students, as they were shaking off the snow, that some of the reading might feel like walking through a blizzard. Everyone chuckled and seemed to quickly get comfortable in spite of wet shoes and cold hands. I explained that I was running this class as a seminar and would like their input as much as possible. I cautioned that if there were strong differences of opinion, I would require that respect be shown for each others' ideas. I also noted that while I would always allow students to express their various perspectives, those perspectives would have to be based on a careful reading of the material.

Not long after the usual introductions and some hot coffee, we settled down and I gave a forty-five minute lecture from Hegel to Heidegger, with a special end-run on Kant. When I saw their eyes beginning to glaze over, I decided to talk about the assignment for the next week. I noted that the photocopied material I had given them would be the starting point for next week's discussion. The students began shuffling through the photocopied excerpts from Plato's *Phaedrus* and *The Sophist* and Aristotle's *Rhetoric*. (The readings had not been included in the initial syllabus.)

One young woman, Belinda, who had introduced herself as a French major, looked puzzled. She mumbled and gave a large sigh. I asked her if there was a problem and she sat quietly for a moment.

Then, leaning forward, elbows on the table, she announced, "I refuse to read any of those white, male, patriarchal misogynists."

The class of sixteen, mostly women, began to stir and nod approvingly. By now, Belinda's face had taken on that "so, lady — what-are-you-going-to-do-about-it" look. Sweat began to trickle down my body.

Authority is always an issue in the classroom, particularly in adult education and in the field of theory and philosophy (which, as a department or discipline, has not had many women as authority figures). I thought I had everything covered. After all, I am a woman, a feminist, and — excuse me for saying so — an open-minded person. I try to be secure enough to "share the power" with students, to use the current pedagogical vernacular. I had not, however, anticipated this reaction.

I had taught for enough years now to know I couldn't let the students smell my fear of mutiny or I would be dead. So I took a deep breath and started my "you have to know the enemy" speech.

After a few sentences, she interrupted, "I think the enemy only gains power when you acknowledge them. If you don't read them, they become irrelevant."

"But," I countered, "this course is based on philosophical issues often defined by Plato and Aristotle, if only to tear them down."

Belinda's face remained defiant. I assigned the readings again and asked her in particular to read "The Allegory of the Cave" in The Republic and to see if she felt corrupted by the text (a ploy I have often used with reluctant students — seeing if they could prove their theory.)

She was having none of it. Quite logically, she retorted, "If I read it then it's too late."

"Well, try anyway, just for the sake of the class," I cajoled. "A sort of experiment in resistance."

At the end of the session, as I started to walk over and talk with her, another student asked a question and Belinda left before I could speak with her.

Session II: The evening of the second class meeting brought more snow. After everyone was settled and beginning to dry off and thaw, I began the class with a shorthand version of the issues surrounding contemporary criticism. Belinda sat directly across from me. I asked the students to point out passages in the reading that they thought were particularly relevant to our discussion and to read them out loud. The fourth student to read chose a passage from "The Allegory of the Cave" and noted two ways in which it reflected the issues in contemporary criticism.

I looked at Belinda and asked if she had a different opinion. She sighed. Then she said, in a loud voice, that she had not read the excerpt. The class seemed motionless, suspended, waiting for my response.

During the previous week I had decided that I was not going to change Belinda's attitude immediately. If she showed up for the second class, however, I would consider that a signal that she was at least willing to listen. Therefore, I had decided to read portions of "The Allegory of the

Cave" to the class.

Rather than confront Belinda about reading the assignment, I began to read and discuss some passages. Belinda sat in class with a decided air of resentment.

Next, I had the students form small groups to discuss the reading more thoroughly and come up with some more questions or points of discussion for the entire class. Belinda's group of four came up with particularly good questions, but without any input from Belinda.

At break, well within earshot of the other students, I commented to her on how well her group performed.

She replied, "I know what you are doing and I think it's manipulation."

"Well, yes of sorts," I said. "I guess all teaching could be considered a manipulation of ideas. A lot of persuasion is necessary — that's true."

Straightening her back, Belinda interrupted, "You see, there you are, you do the manipulating and I do the listening."

"But Belinda, why didn't you just drop the course or leave the room if you felt you were being deprived of your freedom?"

"Oh, right," she sputtered. "Right. I go out of the classroom, you continue as if nothing happened and I have to deal with finding a new class and being behind in it. Right, just what I need! And besides, I wanted to take this class for a reason, but you've never asked me why it's important to me or the history I have with these works."

"Okay, Belinda, tell me what your history is."

"For one thing, I've already seen what they've done, so I don't need to read these guys and I resent your reading them to the class. Furthermore, there are no people of color here."

"Belinda, you read the course description, didn't you? 'These guys,' as you put it, are part of this class, and that's just the way it is — period."

The break was over, but the frustrations voiced in our

conversation hovered during the rest of the class, along with Belinda's icy stare, which seemed to blend into the winter weather outside.

Intermediate Questions:
1. What was the primary difficulty between the teacher and the student?
2. What, if anything, could the teacher have done to avoid the conflict from the beginning?
3. Should the teacher have handled the situation more privately? Less privately?
4. What suggestion would you offer for handling the next class meeting?

Session III: I made my way to the next session though another snowfall. Once inside, I shook off the snow and trudged to the front of the room. Before beginning the session, I motioned for Belinda to come talk to me. I asked her if I could reiterate some of our conversation to the class and see what solution they would offer.

"Sure," was her only response.

For the next forty-five minutes, the class discussed the power relationship between teacher and student, the effects of reading on our lives, and the cultural and racial inadequacies of the canon. This discussion provided Belinda a large forum for her "history" with this material.

As the weeks passed, Belinda added a great deal to the class, albeit reluctantly. Her humor and opinions helped give the class a distinct personality — a condition teachers always hope to attain. Although opening the problems of Belinda and myself to the class did not end the conflict, it began an awareness on everyone's part that criticism can help create a more open classroom.

Final Questions:
1. Do you agree with the instructor's approach to this situation?
2. What are the potential benefits and pitfalls of this ap-

proach?

3. Do any alternate approaches seem more advisable?

4. The next time this instructor teaches this course, what would you suggest she do differently?

The Crush

Carsi Richards Hughes

I quickly swiped the fire-sunset lipstick across my mouth before entering the classroom for fear my naturally pale pink lips would hinder my teaching skill. A feeling of panic surfaced as I wondered what the students would think of me. After all, in addition to being a new instructor, I anticipated being much younger than most of the adult students in my class. I was a twenty-five-year-old clinical psychology graduate student with very little direct teaching experience. Anxiety over my youthfulness was exacerbated by my topic: Geriatric Psychology. I envisioned a classroom of older adults, wrinkled with life experience and wisdom, continually objecting to my so-called knowledge of those over age 65. The least I could do, I thought, is wear some lipstick to increase my professionalism.

But lipstick was only the beginning. To further compensate for my naivete, I spent a great deal of time refining my style and classroom techniques. For example, I was always prompt and courteous, even on days when I'd rather be anywhere but in a hot classroom. I perfected my humor and (with only a few exceptions) could induce laughter at any given time. Of course I also boned up on my knowledge of geriatrics so that I was seldom asked a question I couldn't clearly and simply explain. I often elaborated upon topics with interesting examples gleaned from my clinical and personal experiences. In fact, I often referred to my husband and his family in my examples (particularly when looking for appropriate examples of severe psychopathology!). I even allowed for a partial discussion of my initial syllabus and made a few changes based upon class feedback. In sum, I desperately wanted to be seen as a competent, good-natured, entertaining, open instructor and made great effort to appear as such.

To add to these already nearly super-human efforts, I decided to make more time for my students individually.

The decision was partly selfish: for me, it was much more comfortable engaging in one-on-one discourse as opposed to pontificating for a crowd. Plus, individual interactions allowed me to notice the diversity in my class and challenge some of my original stereotypes. For example, my fear of being endlessly heckled by a group of older adults was wholly unfounded. My students' ages ranged from twenty-six to sixty-two with the average age being approximately 35. Not quite the geriatric bunch I'd been visualizing. When students had questions or needed help, I tried to make myself available as much as possible and at their convenience. Sometimes we'd meet before or after class or during a break. I gave out my telephone number and helped several students by telephone between class times. The students appeared to benefit from the extra time and attention. I could see them putting an enormous amount of energy into their assignments and feeling satisfied with their work. Overall, I was pleased.

One student, Jamie, did not seem to respond to me in class or one-on-one. This student, a male in his late 20s, couldn't complete his assignments in a timely manner, even with substantial encouragement. Although Jamie came to class every week, he always sat in the back. He appeared to pay attention to lectures (he even laughed at my jokes) but did not participate unless I asked him a direct question. Even then his remarks were abbreviated, and he could not sustain eye contact. Occasionally he would have a conversation with another student but would become silent when I walked by. Individually, he was even more perplexing. He would distract himself from our conversations and nervously tap his feet. Believing that his attitude must be directly related to my teaching prowess, I became increasingly motivated to see him do well in the course. Then I began to wonder: maybe he just didn't like me. What could he possibly not like about me? Was it my demeanor? My style? My lipstick? I then began an all-out effort to help this student with his assignments, thereby proving, on some level that

he actually DID like me and that I was not a failure as an
instructor. Toward this end, I was willing to try anything.
First, I gave him space. I did not call upon him in class. I
did not force him to meet with me privately. That did not
seem to change the situation, so I changed my strategy: I
made a point of saying hello to him without asking about
his assignments. I required him to meet with me individually. As a clinical psych grad student, I couldn't resist thinking about him in an analytical way. I cautiously began to
move toward asking him more about his personal life.
Maybe, just maybe, he was having problems at home or in
his social life that were keeping him from full classroom
participation. Maybe it wasn't his dislike of me after all! I
recall beaming with newfound hope and secretly hoping that
this young man's behavior was rooted in domestic disturbance. I could hardly wait to see him again to confirm my
hypothesis.

That day, Jamie had left a small package for me in my
mailbox. Enclosed were several articles about Alzheimer's
disease he had clipped from the newspaper. Attached was a
personal note that read:

> This might seem silly, but I have a crush on you
> that has progressed throughout the semester. Your
> personality, appearance, humor, and intelligence have
> made it difficult for me to concentrate. I'm hoping
> that this is not fruitless. Can't wait to see you again.
>
> Jamie.

I was shocked. Here I am, I thought, a married woman
desperately trying for respect as a new instructor, and somehow a student has a crush on me. How sophomoric! How
demeaning! And then it occurred to me: had I fueled this
crush? Had I wanted so desperately to be liked that I crossed
the boundaries of instructor and student? Was my lipstick
too provocative for a young, single male? Most importantly,
what would I do at the next class? Would I continue to see

him alone? Should I "process" this with him?

The following week, dressed in boyish trousers and a loose-fitting shirt, I sprinted into class only seconds before it began. I gave my lecture without my usual smiles. I referred to my husband and his family repeatedly. I made no eye contact with Jamie or anyone else for that matter. I apologetically cancelled my individual meetings for that day and quickly left after class. Driving home that night, I felt a sense of relief that I had avoided Jamie. I also knew that, eventually, I would have to deal with the situation. I took a week to think about the situation. Yes, I had given the students individual attention. Yes, I wanted them all to enjoy my teaching and to like me. Yes, I was dynamic and silly and perhaps over-involved with the class. Definitely over-involved with Jamie. However, I was never flirtatious. I was not attracted to Jamie. I had no intentions of leading him on and, quite honestly, was not even flattered by his note. I was angry with him for seeing me as a potential date rather than respecting my intellect and teaching ability. I was angry with myself for needing others' approval to such an extent that I would contribute to a situation like this. With these conclusions in mind, I was ready to meet with Jamie.

After the next class, I asked to see Jamie alone. Before I could offer any reactions to his note or to the obvious awkward feelings between us, he spoke. Jamie informed me that he had not meant for the note to disrupt the flow of the class. He was aware that I was married. He was aware that nothing would come of his confession. He hoped that I was flattered and that we could put the whole thing behind us for the rest of the semester.

"You were flattered, at least, weren't you?" Jamie asked hesitatingly.

"Of course," I lied, "of course."

Questions:

1. What might the instructor have done to ensure that this situation would not arise?

2. What might the instructor have done differently once the crush was revealed?
3. What degree of teacher/student socializing is acceptable in an adult education setting?
4. Should a teacher and student socialize during a semester? After a semester is over, if the student continues to be enrolled in the program?

A Case of Dislike
Robert Fromberg

On the first day of class she was late. Professor Hughes could not remember any student making a bigger production of being inconspicuous when entering a classroom late. She hunched her shoulders and scurried along the perimeter of the room, staying close to the wall, seeming to put on a show of bravery against the vicissitudes of fate that delayed her and the ignominy of entering the class after the instructor had begun speaking. Professor Hughes wondered, as he went through the pro forma first-night-of-class announcements, how a person who apparently is upset and in a great hurry could manage to keep her hair looking so perfect. He had never been able to manage that feat. He smiled to himself as he continued with the announcements; she needn't be so upset about being late. He didn't care if a person were late to class, as long as it didn't happen regularly.

She was settling into a seat in the corner as he finished the announcements. He asked her name to compare it to the class list, and she looked up, blinked twice, and told him in a shaky voice. She did not speak again all night—the only student in the eighteen-member class who did not join in an informal discussion about celebrities on television that Professor Hughes was using to make a point about the importance of detail in descriptive writing.

The title of the class was intermediate composition, a class Professor Hughes had taught every semester for the previous six years. He was an adjunct faculty member, teaching four or five classes per year—two classes in the fall and spring semesters and often one in the summer. In addition to intermediate composition, Professor Hughes taught other creative and expository writing classes, along with an occasional introductory literature course. He enjoyed teaching, and what he enjoyed most about it was the students. Writing and literature were dear subjects to him, and exciting to discuss, but even more than he enjoyed those subjects, he enjoyed the friendly, enthusiastic, and always surprising students and their equally engaging writing and class discussion.

When he first had begun teaching at the university, he had worked full-time during the day in a corporate environment as a writer and editor. When he left to pursue freelance writing, he had been concerned that he would miss the camaraderie of the workplace, but the camaraderie of the classroom had filled the gap nicely. Now, even though he was busier than ever, he looked forward to class as his chance to be with people he liked.

The student, whose name was Jennifer, was late for the next class meeting, once again making a display of brave forbearance against the pressures of life, or so Professor Hughes thought. He felt a mounting annoyance toward her —more than his usual response to perpetual latecomers. He wasn't sure why he felt so uncharitable toward her. Perhaps it was her perfect hair, artful makeup, and crisp clothes. He found himself wondering, if she had so much time to spend on her appearance, why couldn't she also set aside enough time to arrive at class when the rest of the students did.

And again, Jennifer did not participate in class discussions and exercises. She did pay attention, but appeared a bit perplexed, especially during the less formal discussions.

At the end of class, Jennifer lagged behind as the other students were dropping their first papers on the table in front of the professor. When the others had gone, she began in a breathless voice to explain that she hadn't finished her paper. She had been terribly busy at work, she said, both of her children were sick, and her baby-sitter had suddenly quit. She continued, explaining that she was a single working mother and was having difficulty fitting in school as well but that everything should be better soon.

As she spoke, Professor Hughes noticed that her hands trembled. She was truly upset, probably exhausted. He wondered how old she was and guessed she always had been and always would be in her mid-forties, although in reality she was most likely barely past 30. He wanted to stop her in the middle of this stream of excuses, but couldn't break her momentum. Finally she paused, and he said, "No problem. Those are all excellent reasons to turn in a paper late. Just give it to me next time."

"But," she had continued, "your syllabus says that the grade is lowered when the paper is late."

He waved that away. "Don't worry about that. That's just to cover myself when people constantly turn in papers late."

He had decided not to mention her tardiness—she did seem to have much to juggle in her life—but she brought it up herself. "I'm really sorry about being late last week and this week, but this is the busiest time of year in my work. The restaurant I manage does a lot of lunch and afternoon events, and often I don't get finished until late afternoon, and I have to pick up my daughter from school, and then I'm way out in the suburbs and the traffic coming down-town is always terrible...."

"Is this going to be a problem all semester?"

"Oh, no, this should be the last bad week; after that I'll have everything straightened out. I'll be in class on time and I'll have my papers in on time. I swear."

Professor Hughes found himself both sad and annoyed that this person with two children and a business would seem so frightened of him. He had always tried—and suc-ceeded, he thought—to avoid being a figure of authority.

"Okay, no problem," he said, waving away her tardi-ness as he had her late paper. "You've obviously got a lot to cope with. I don't want to make you even more harried than you are."

She was absent the next class period. Professor Hughes was annoyed. Well, he thought, I gave her one break, but that may be the last one. At break he checked both his mail-box and his voice mail, but she had left him no message.

After class that evening, Professor Hughes walked to his home—a high-rise apartment near campus—and two hours later was about to head for bed when the telephone rang. It was the doorman, saying a woman named Jennifer was downstairs, wanting to see him.

Professor Hughes said he would be right down, slipped on some shoes, and headed for the elevator. In the lobby, Jennifer was pacing, a manila envelope in her hand. When she saw him, she approached, talking quickly.

"I'm sorry to come so late, but I've been stopping at all the apartment buildings in the area. I remembered your saying that you'd recently moved to a high-rise near school, and you weren't in the phone book, but I figured I could find it if I just drove around and looked at all the directories. I'm sorry I wasn't in class, but I had a miserable day yesterday; I was up almost all night—in fact, that's what I wrote about in my paper—and it took until now to get my paper written."

She paused to hand Professor Hughes the envelope. He glanced at the door. As he took it from her, he said, "You really could have just left the paper in my mailbox at school. Or mailed it to me at school."

"Oh, but it was already a week late and I wanted to make sure you got it today... ."

As Jennifer continued talking, he slipped the essay out of the envelope. The paper felt heavier than the five pages he had assigned. He turned to the end and saw the number on the last page was eight. Next he noticed the typeface—so small it was difficult to read. And the paper was not double-spaced—the one mechanical requirement he had insisted on when giving instructions. The margins were almost nonexistent.

"Jennifer," Professor Hughes said, interrupting her, "this paper is much longer than what I'd assigned."

"Oh, I hoped you wouldn't notice. I tried to squeeze it into as few pages as possible."

"I'm just concerned because you're making more work

for yourself."

"Oh, but the subject had to be that long. It's the story of what happened to me yesterday night, you just wouldn't believe... ."

The doorman was sitting just a few feet away taking this all in. Professor Hughes was aware of the doorman, of the late hour, and of his growing vexation with this entire situation. He waited for an opening and told Jennifer he had to go back upstairs and would see her next week. She started to tell him more about her paper, and he listened until she paused, then, again, told her he would talk to her next week. She asked about the next assignment, and despite his increasing irritation, he went over the guidelines with her, reminding her to stay within the length limits, if only to cut down on the work she had to do. After what seemed an eternity, he escaped back upstairs.

The paper was a disaster, or at least that's the word Professor Hughes found in his mind while reading. The sentences were long and unwieldy, the grammar and spelling were inconsistent, and the scenes were described in an absurd level of detail, as though she were terrified she might leave out something important. But what really bothered Professor Hughes was what he considered near-racist depictions. The essay, a narrative, involved being stranded in a stalled car and featured descriptions of threatening black men and a Hispanic tow-truck driver who offered to trade the cost of the towing for sex. Professor Hughes marked these passages in hard, angry strokes of his pen.

After reading the paper, he wrote out comments on a separate sheet. Normally he tried to start his comments with strengths of the writing, but this time he didn't bother. He noted the technical problems, as well as problems of style and lack of selectivity. He suggested they meet to discuss the essay.

"I almost dropped the class when I saw your comments and the way you marked up my essay," she said when they sat down to meet over a week later. In the interim she had attended class, arriving on time, but again did not participate in the discussion.

Professor Hughes was surprised at her reaction to his grading, but when he glanced down at the corrected paper, he understood immediately. His blue marks were everywhere, correcting technique, questioning content. And he knew the comments he had written on the cover sheet, while valid, were tinged with his annoyance and offered little support.

"Yes," he said, "I guess I can see what you mean. It's easy to forget how it feels to have someone write all over your work. Perhaps I could have found another way to correct the paper. However, the writing does have some difficulties we need to discuss."

He picked one of the more unwieldy sentences, and they discussed how it could be changed, making very little progress. "You just don't like long sentences," she said. "I think we just have a different style."

He tried to point out that the sentence contained grammatical mistakes, and those were what he wanted to correct. Sensing they were at a dead end, he picked a different sentence, but before they could begin dissecting it, Jennifer pointed to another passage on the same page. It was one of the racial characterizations he had marked. "I didn't understand your comment here. What's wrong with this? That's what actually happened."

He tried to explain the difficulties in the passage, but she did not seem to understand his interpretation. When the meeting ended, Professor Hughes wondered how this situation had soured so badly and so quickly. In the past, he had had students who had serious writing problems, and in most cases he and the student had been able to amicably work on the difficulties. He frequently also had students who overextended themselves, whose work and other commitments resulted in late assignments and more absences than Professor Hughes would like to see. In most cases, he and the students had worked out an acceptable compromise. He knew he did not like this student, but he had to admit her life seemed quite taxing. She talked about a recent divorce, business problems, a custody battle. Perhaps he should give her a break of some sort, but he honestly did not want to. Yet he did not want her to fail or drop the class. Surely he could figure a way to change the mood, momentum, and direction; surely he could find a way to put this relationship back on course.

Questions:
1. What was Professor Hughes' earliest misstep? What other wrong steps did he take?
2. What does this situation suggest about the responsibilities of instructors and of students, especially working students?
3. What could Professor Hughes do now to improve this situation?
4. Should Professor Hughes try to improve the situation?
5. What could Professor Hughes change in the way his class is conducted to avoid these difficulties in the future without harming the successful elements of his teaching?

The Dominating Auditor
Laurence D. Schiller

The Setting:
This case takes place in the continuing education school of a Midwestern university. The students range in age from approximately twenty-two to sixty-five and attend classes for a variety of reasons. Some are seeking bachelor's or master's degrees or certificates necessary to change careers or advance in their present positions, while other students simply seek instruction in a particular subject and are less concerned with class credit. In addition, some students audit certain courses rather than participate for a grade. Tuition for auditors is approximately 50 percent less than the rate for students. Most of the instructors are employed outside the university and teach one or two courses per semester. Nearly all of the classes meet only one evening per week for two to three hours.

The Problem:
Mike registered to audit a survey class on the Middle East. For that semester, the course would include a detailed examination of the Arab-Israeli conflict. The class had nearly twenty-five students all of whom were "full-freight" students except for Mike.

At first Mike felt he shouldn't say much in class because he was not participating for a grade, but that quickly faded when he felt the instructor was not addressing the areas about which he sought more information. He had paid for this course and his time was very valuable, so he wanted to get the most out of the class.

He began to ask questions that challenged what he felt was a misguided effort by members of the Middle-East peace movement in Israel to pacify terrorists. He told the class that it would endanger the continued existence of Israel if the government were to give up the Golan Heights and grant

Palestinians self-rule in Gaza and the West Bank.

Mike brought in pamphlets that gave a side of the story he thought the instructor, Mr. Jones, was not providing. He often interrupted Mr. Jones to share his opinion, usually without even raising his hand. He noticed other students rolling their eyes or shaking their heads when he spoke or brought articles for Mr. Jones to share with the class, but he hoped that he would shed some light on why Israel's government has behaved as it has and how he, and many other Jews like him, thought it should continue to react.

In his previous classes, Mr. Jones always encouraged class participation. He believes students learn more if they are involved, so he invites questions from the class. Sometimes he even asks students to try to answer each other's questions. He also knows the subject matter is very difficult to understand and he doesn't want to be one of those instructors who never takes the time to make sure the entire class really understands what he is telling them.

But this semester he became increasingly more reluctant to seek out questions from this class because he felt that Mike always tried to dominate the discussion and would draw him off on tangents. He could sense the rest of the class becoming more passive and merely taking notes rather than getting involved. He began to feel that Mike was an intrusion and should sit back and listen since he was only auditing the course. Mr. Jones was also concerned about the rising hostility in the class toward Mike, and it appeared to him that some of the students were now transferring their anger to him as the instructor.

About Mike:

Mike was a forty-five-year-old accountant. His family had emigrated to the United States from Germany just before the Nazis took power in the 1930s. He was a devout Jew who wanted to learn more about the conflicts in Israel. He firmly believed Israel was the promised land and that the Jewish people had the right to govern the region, which includes using that force necessary to protect the country's citizens and its borders.

Through stories his parents told him as a child, Mike knew all too well the dangers of anti-semitism. He was most troubled by the growing sentiment in the United States that Israel should return the Golan Heights to Syria and give Palestinians the power of self-rule.

Mike had heard numerous rabbis and historians speak on the issue, but he never felt he really understood the conflict between the Arabs and Israelis in the region. He was ambivalent about returning to college with a bunch of eighteen-year-olds merely to take one or two history courses, especially considering the long hours he usually worked, but auditing a class for adults seemed like a reasonable alternative. He would not have to devote too much time to course work and the financial commitment was minimal, yet still he would have all of the resources of a major university, including highly qualified instructors, at his fingertips.

About Bob Jones:

Mr. Jones works full-time for a newsletter that deals with economic and social issues in the Middle East. He has taught history at the university for a number of years. His favorite class to teach is this course because it is such a "hot-button" topic, and it has always engendered lively class discussion.

The class sessions are only 2½ hours after breaks are figured in. As far as Mr. Jones is concerned, that is barely enough time to get warmed up, let alone do any real justice to such highly charged issues as the conflicts in the Middle East. Mr. Jones has always tried to stick to a very regimented outline to fit what he considers necessary material into this limited time slot.

The Problem Gets Worse:

One particular session Mr. Jones began the evening as he always did by asking if anyone had any questions about the material covered last week. A few people raised their hands, including Mike. Mr. Jones pointed to each student who then asked his or her question. Mr. Jones tried to answer the questions in a brief one- or two-minute dissertation. Then, reluctantly, he pointed to Mike.

"What is the incentive for Israel to deal with states that don't recognize the existence of Israel and sponsor terrorism?" Mike asked.

Even though this question had nothing to do with the material covered during the previous meeting and was unrelated to the subject matter of that evening's lecture, Mr. Jones tried to answer the question. He thought he gave a fairly non-judgmental response giving both sides of the issue, but he also rushed through the subject because he wanted to move on to the evening's topic. Mike felt the answer was too superficial and wanted to know more, so without raising his hand, he asked a follow up question.

"Professor, Israel has tried to trust its 'neighbors' on three different occasions and each time we had to go to war, so why should we trust them now? Simply because President George Bush asked us to during the Gulf War, and now President Clinton asks the same?"

Some of the students started to whisper and a few grumbles were audible. Mr. Jones asked if anyone in the class could answer Mike's question. One woman spoke up pointing out that Israel was responsible for starting the Six-Day War.

"We had to defend ourselves against terrorism. Innocent people are killed every year simply because they're Jews." Mike's face was flushed and he was practically yelling.

"Shut up already," another student muttered partly under his breath loud enough for everyone to hear.

"We need to move on with tonight's discussion about Syria's relations with the other Arab countries," Mr. Jones said quickly.

A couple of students closed their books, others shifted

uncomfortably in their seats. No one participated in the rest of the evening's lecture and Mr. Jones did not attempt to engage the students in a discussion about the subject.

Questions:
1. What are some of the ways Mr. Jones could deal with the fact that Mike seemed to be dominating class discussions?
2. How do you address tangential questions without being rude? What if the questions seem to incite hostility in the other students?
3. How should an instructor address important, but sensitive topics? How do you encourage full discussion without allowing any one student to dominate?
4. How should the instructor keep the class on track without cutting off all opportunities for class discussion?
5. Should students leave some of their personal beliefs and notions at home, only discussing the topics at hand based upon the materials and instruction provided?
6. What should an instructor do if a student seems to be pushing his or her own agenda in class?
7. Should an instructor permit an auditor to participate in class on the same level as other students? Should an auditor expect to be able to participate fully in class?

The Group that Couldn't Keep Up
Kurt Cogswell

Mack is an advanced graduate student in math. He is teaching an intensive summer calculus course which meets for three hours an evening, five nights a week. He struggled into his heavy backpack and hopped on his bike, relieved to be heading home after the last class meeting. As he pedaled toward his apartment, the sweet night air enveloped him. He reflected back on the last few weeks, thinking that teaching a quarter of introductory calculus to a diverse group of students in four weeks can be an interesting experience, in the sense of the well-known Chinese curse, "May you live in interesting times."

Mack's class consisted of fifteen very diverse students, including five adults returning to professional programs in the fall, and two hot-shot high school students who had already burned through their high schools' curricula. The grueling summer-school condensed schedule had been a mind-numbing experience, for even the most motivated student.

Mack's preferred method of teaching math had always been to minimize lecture and maximize small-group interaction while he circulated around the room. He felt that approach became a virtual necessity, especially when the alternative was three hours of lecture punctuated by small breaks. He preferred to let the groups self-select when possible. In the course that had just concluded, he realized that mostly due to blind luck in the students' initial seating choices, he was able to arrange the groups so that each contained one of the adult students. He reasoned that these were the people most likely to have rusty fundamental skills from disuse and correspondingly high levels of math anxiety. His hope was that the younger students could help the older ones over the rough spots in their fundamentals, while the older students could supply the high level of motivation necessary to get through such an intense course.

This theory worked beautifully in four of the five groups. He believed he could even claim that most of these people had fun during what could have been a rough four weeks. The fifth group, on the other hand, was a disappointment. It had consisted of three students: Kelly, a woman returning to school — an MBA program — after several years away from academics; Joyce, a nineteen or twenty year old college sophomore; and Angela, a high school junior.

Kelly was extremely nervous about tackling calculus under such difficult circumstances, but had no choice in the matter because it was a requirement for her MBA. Joyce was trying to make up for lost time after switching from a music major to an engineering major after her freshman year. Angela was a special case. Very bright, hard-working, and motivated (she plans to win a Nobel prize in medicine one day), she also has congenital birth defects that make her speech and movements slow, labored, and spasmodic.

Within the first several class meetings, Mack noticed that, despite her obvious high level of accomplishment, Angela had a severe lack of self-confidence. She would announce, in a loud, overbearing way, her frustration with the course material and her belief that she was "slowing down the group." She would follow these outbursts with equally intense apologies. As a high school student, Mack knew it must have been extremely difficult for her be the youngest in the class. True, there was another high schooler, but he was socially adept and seemed to blend in easily with the other students, regardless of age.

Despite her youth, Angela had much to offer both Joyce and Kelly, but Mack knew it would take a good deal of patience and understanding on their parts to gain the benefit. Although Joyce might have had the necessary patience and understanding, unfortunately Kelly seemed to have little of either. She would fidget and occasionally even drum her fingers on her desk when Angela began to speak. Usually this frustration showed during Angela's bouts of self-doubt, but Kelly often seemed impatient when Angela was making a valuable contribution to an exercise. This impatience was exacerbated by Kelly's difficulties absorbing the complex material. She seemed to want an instructor to give her "the answer." Instead, she found herself sitting among several students — one with some physical and emotional difficulties — struggling her way through difficult problems.

While Joyce didn't show such overt signs of frustration, neither was she showing a command of calculus. And her fellow group members were not able to offer much immediate assistance.

During the first few sessions, Mack spent almost half of his circulating time with Angela, Kelly, and Joyce's group. Unfortunately, even that close attention seemed insufficient to bolster Angela's sagging ego and to help Kelly and Joyce understand the basics of calculus. However, he felt he could not spend all his time with that one group. He worried that he was giving short shrift to the others.

By the seventh (out of twenty) class meeting, it was clear that there were four outstanding group collaborations and one potential disaster. Mack pondered his options. He could split up Angela, Kelly, and Joyce, placing each in one of the more successful groups. However, Angela would have inevitably taken that as a personal defeat, heaping blame on her own shoulders. Kelly and Joyce may have benefited from being placed in other groups, but the other groups were working too well to risk tinkering with their success.

Mack decided to speak with Kelly outside of class. He offered to do all that he could to help her through the class. Also, he discussed her obvious impatience with Angela, trying to enlist her as a compatriot in his attempts to bolster Angela's confidence. She agreed to give it a try.

As the condensed quarter wore on, Mack and Kelly met twice outside of class, but that time was not sufficient to give her the help she needed. Finding time for outside-class meetings was no easy task! Class met for three hours, five nights a week, and Mack was also busy writing his dissertation and working days in the bookstore.

Kelly's frustration with Angela cooled somewhat, and Joyce seemed to gain comfort with the small-group format, but the group was not a happy collaboration. Mack continued to spend more time with that group than with any of the others, although he couldn't escape the feeling that he was cheating the other groups to some extent.

Almost before he knew it, the four-week "quarter" was over. His course evaluations contained fourteen glowing reviews and one scathing review of the small-group concept. He rated the class a success, and, he thought, as he rode home under the summer star-filled sky, I believe I did the best I thought possible.

However, he still had second (and third and fourth) thoughts about how he might have handled the situation.

Questions:

1. What could the instructor have done to change the dynamic of the struggling group?
2. What changes could the instructor have made in the class structure as a whole to accommodate the struggling group without hurting the others?
3. Was the small group format appropriate for this class?
4. Must an instructor accept that a certain percentage of students in any class will not succeed? At what point does an instructor accept such a situation?
5. How could the instructor have better dealt with the differences in age, experience, and knowledge among the class?
6. Are such intensive classes advisable? In general, what can an instructor do to make them more tolerable?

A Case of Culture Shock
Robert Fromberg

I had used the tape before. In fact, I had used the tape in all of my women's studies classes and also in some of my introduction to sociology classes for the past four years or so. I might soon have to replace the tape with a more current performance, but I had never considered changing the basic teaching technique.

The tape got a great response in my traditional day-school undergraduate courses. I knew that on the first day when the students saw me heading toward that videotape player they expected the worst: some turgid documentary featuring droning scholars. When the tape rolled and suddenly pop-music idol Madonna appeared on the television screen—well! I could almost feel the sense of combined relief and surprise and delight. Talk about starting a class on the right note! I'm sure they were at least relieved that their teacher, despite a few gray hairs and sensible walking shoes, wasn't an old fogy.

A few of the students might exchange glances, might look a little uncomfortable at first, but often these turned out to be students who didn't participate much in class anyway and often seemed uncomfortable with the honesty of our discussions. And a few of the students in the last couple of years have said something about Madonna being old hat (although I don't think that was the phrase they used), but they seemed happy to join in the discussion.

Of course, most of the "traditional" students knew the Madonna performance well, but playing it for the group put the details freshly in the kids' minds. The discussions that followed usually were superb. In the women's studies classes, the Madonna videotape elicited instant response on many of the key topics in the course: the nature of power and sexuality for women, the depiction of women in the media, and much more. Sometimes the responses caused conflicts: some students were passionate in their disapproval or their approval of Madonna and her performance. Yet I had always been able to channel the conflict into a productive discussion of the conflicting desires and responsibilities, internal and external pressures inherent in being a woman in this country today.

In my introduction to sociology courses, I used the tape in a more limited fashion, just trying to introduce the idea that isolated examples of public behavior, such as this music video, carried elements of collective societal beliefs and habits. Discussion of the videotape in these classes was usually a bit more subdued than in the women's studies classes, but was nonetheless productive.

In my evening classes, which were almost exclusively women's studies classes, the responses were similar — but not identical — to those in the day classes. The students were virtually all women, and they ranged in age from the late twenties to as old as seventy. The younger students tended to hold jobs like administrative assistant or sales clerk as they pursued their degrees at night. The middle-aged students tended to be professionals, mothers, or both; some were pursuing a degree, while others were there just for the pleasure of learning. The oldest students tended not to be pursuing a degree, but were mostly there to learn and for the social interaction.

I taught approximately two evening classes per year and had done so for the past four or five years. The Madonna video was almost as good an icebreaker for the evening classes as for the day classes. The younger evening students knew all about Madonna and were conversant in the issues she epitomized. The middle-aged students sometimes shook their heads in dismay at the overtly sexual display on the screen, but usually had a few intelligent words to say, although they tended to carry a mildly judgmental tone. The subtext seemed to be something like, "She wouldn't have time to cavort around if she had a real job and kids."

I had only had two or three students over 60 in all my

evening classes combined — certainly not enough to draw any firm conclusions about how women in that age group react to Madonna. As I recall, one of the older women had strong, intelligent comments to make, and the other one or two were pretty quiet, but were also quiet during most of our discussions pertaining to sexuality or sexual relationships.

The fall semester was about to begin for the evening program. I planned to play the tape on the first night of class and to ask students to write a three-page reaction. The paper was to begin with a personal, gut-level response and then move toward the larger societal issues represented by the personal, visceral response.

The class makeup was about the usual mix of younger, middle-aged, and older students, and their reaction when I rolled the tape was pretty typical. The younger students seemed pleased to have their stereotypes about scholarship undercut, the middle-aged students appeared bemused and a bit uncomfortable, and the one older student looked on impassively. Afterwards, we discussed the tape, with the same issues as usual arising, and I made my assignment. I went home that night thinking more about a research project I was conducting than about the just-completed class session.

However, the next afternoon my office phone rang and I found the associate dean of the evening program on the line and sounding a bit more formal than usual.

The older student from last night had called the dean to complain. She found the Madonna performance to be entirely inappropriate for the classroom. In particular, she was offended by a scene in which Madonna, with large protruding cones over her breasts, simulated a sex act.

"I have to tell you," said the dean, "that the student made her points well. She wasn't infuriated, she just thought the tape was needlessly vulgar and that you could have made the points another way. She said she wouldn't write the paper and has dropped the class."

I was dumbfounded. I had always gotten reasonably good

responses on my student evaluations, and I had never had a student complain about me — at least, not to my knowledge.

I hemmed and hawed, trying to get my thoughts in order. "Well," I said, "I know that the video is a bit shocking, but I think that's good—it makes people sit up and pay attention, and it gets discussion going, and it shows people that the class will involve some honest discussion." I was starting to gather speed. "Maybe the most important point is that learning should involve some discomfort. That's the feeling people have when their mental and emotional models are being broken, and that's what learning is all about."

The dean asked about the content of the video, whether I had used it in the past, and what the reaction had been. Finally he said, "We need to consider the makeup of the evening classes, the diverse backgrounds and experiences. And we always need to look at our teaching methods and materials with that audience in mind. We need to carefully assess whether the potential benefit for one group of our students outweighs any potential adverse effect on other students. I don't say you should never challenge a class; I realize that's one way learning takes place. But perhaps you should consider working your way up to something like Madonna. Is the shock value really that important?"

I said I would certainly consider these points and would call the dean back later in the week to discuss them further. I asked for the student's phone number, thinking I could explain the rationale for the videotape to her. However, the dean said he had already asked the student whether she wanted to talk about the class with me, and the student had declined, preferring simply to drop.

After I hung up, I was tempted to shake my head and say, "There's one in every crowd." But I couldn't put the disgruntled student out of my mind so easily.

Questions:
1. Can a good instructor expect to never have a disgruntled student?

2. Is this student's complaint merely an isolated incident, or does it signal some larger difficulty with this instructor's approach to teaching?
3. To what extent should an instructor let diverse ages and backgrounds shape teaching methods and materials?
4. Assess this instructor's ideas about and approaches to "breaking mental and emotional models."
5. Do you suggest this instructor modify her approach to the evening classes? If so, how? Do these modifications also have implications for her day-school classes?

The Case of the Bewildered Student
John Jacob

"That's a pretty good start for the first class. We still have about ten minutes left, but let's take off early tonight. Read the essays and the chapter in the handbook about development, and remember that we have two research papers in this class, and it isn't too early to start thinking about topics. See you next week. Oh, and don't forget to leave your placement essays behind so I can file them."

As the students started for the door, some talking with one another, the instructor noticed that one woman appeared rooted to her seat. He erased the blackboard and started to gather his books, papers, and placement essays, when he saw the telltale blue cover in her hand and realized that she was still holding onto her essay.

Jack's words at the start of class ran through his mind: "Those of you who wrote placement essays and were put in this class as a result, you should be pleased. Placement in this class means you have mastered many of the basics of expository writing. You can look over the placement essays during our break, and I'll try to answer any questions you may have. Make sure you return the essays after break so I can file them."

Jack approached the woman's desk. "Sorry," he said, "I'm so bad on names, but I'll get them soon. You are...?"

"Pam."

"Right, Pam. I need to pick up the placement essay. Or do you want to discuss it?"

"Um, Professor... ."

"Call me Jack."

"OK, well, it's just that I've looked through this placement essay, and I don't see many marks on it, and I can't figure it out."

"Can't figure out...?"

"Can't figure out why I was placed in this class. I didn't

ask to be placed here, and now that I've sat through the first session, I'm sure it's going to be over my head."

"Well, let me look over the essay. I may not even have been one of the readers originally."

Jack started reading the essay, sometimes squinting to figure out the handwriting. He had been one of the readers, but he remembered the essay only vaguely. After a couple of paragraphs, he glanced up and saw a bead of sweat on Pam's forehead and her lips compressed into a thin line. He glanced back down at the essay. He found it difficult to read the work carefully with her sitting there, especially after a day that had started at six in the morning.

"Pam, I did read the essay before, but along with about fifty others. I wish I remembered it better. I do remember thinking it was written well, organized well. And you can tell by the lack of marks that we didn't find many mechanical or syntactical errors."

"Syn...?"

"Sorry. Syntactical. I mean, the sentence structures were fine. And I thought you explained your point well and developed it with examples. No one even considered placing you in the lower class. Tell me why you think this class is going to be over your head."

"It's just that I've been out of school so long. Ten or eleven years. And I've never been good at writing. I can't even write a letter. And I didn't get very good grades in English class in high school."

"Well, no one likes writing letters these days, and high school was a while ago. You know, I didn't do all that well in high school English — too preoccupied with having fun."

Pam shifted in her seat then rubbed her temple. "Really, I'm just nervous about this class. When you listed all the things we were going to do, it just sounded like so much. I didn't understand the words you were using. Look, I'm just a waitress. The other people in here, they're wearing business clothes — suits, blouses, skirts, pearls — and I probably still smell like grease and coffee."

"I don't know, Pam, I saw a few people in jeans and sweatshirts. And I bet the people in suits wish they were wearing comfortable clothes. But the point is that the way people dress or what they do for a living doesn't mean anything about how smart they are. Look, it's too early to quit. Give it another week. When I see some of your writing I can sit down and talk to you about it, give you a little extra help, though you may think you need more help than you actually do."

"You'd help me like that? Spend a few minutes before class?"

"Sure, no problem."

"Well, could you explain a couple of things you said in class right now?"

Jack's thoughts of getting home a few minutes early, of getting something for his growling stomach, evaporated. "Uh, sure." A half-hour later, they agreed to continue the discussion one hour before class next week.

Before Jack quite knew what was happening, he and Pam seemed to have established a schedule that involved his meeting her for an hour before class every week. She would set up the meeting at the end of each class; during the first five weeks of class, the only time they did not meet was one week he said he had a doctor's appointment (but actually had to catch up on grading papers). Pam's writing was not the best in the class, but it was far from the worst.

The sessions were as productive as could be expected given the limited amount of time. He was able to help her spot several common grammatical errors she made often, as well as reduce the number of cliches in her writing. Of course, more needed to be done; Pam especially needed encouragement to more assertively draw conclusions based on her evidence.

The irony of the situation did not escape Jack: Pam's writing may have lacked assertiveness, but she had no problem staking a claim to his time. By the fifth week, Jack knew that he had to curtail these before-class tutoring sessions. Not only was Pam getting more attention than other students who needed the help more but were less willing to ask for it, but Jack was tiring of rushing to campus early and cramming down a sandwich while he drove so he could meet Pam.

At the end of the fifth class meeting, Pam as usual lagged behind as the others walked toward the door. She approached the desk and asked, "Would you mind talking to me for just a moment about this paper you handed back?"

Jack thought about the page and a half of typed comments he had given her on the paper, more than he had given to any other student—enough, he had hoped, to preclude questions.

"All right," he said, "but, Pam, I have to tell you that starting next week, I have another class I have to teach before this one. It's in the western suburbs, and I'll just barely have time to make it here by class time."

Pam raised her eyebrows.

Jack continued, "And so I guess we'll have to, um, curtail our before-class sessions."

"But we agreed," she said, her voice rising a bit in pitch and volume. "I said I'd take the class, but only if I had help, and you said you'd give me extra time. You can't just abandon me in the middle of the semester. This class still is so hard for me. Just being in school again scares me to death. I don't want to drop out now. It's not just the tuition, although you can't imagine how many tables I have to wait to take this class. It's that I want to do something else with my life besides wait tables."

Jack found himself running his schedule through his mind, looking for an open slot for Pam. Then he shook his head. No, this wasn't right. What if he did this for every student? Or even just for every student apprehensive about returning to school? He'd never have time to sleep or eat, let alone prepare for class.

Having finished her speech, Pam was staring at him

intently, her lips tight as they had been that first night. She wasn't sweating now, but she looked as if she might cry. Without quite knowing what he was going to say, Jack opened his mouth to reply.

Questions:
1. What special considerations can instructors make to help adult students returning to school to overcome fears and adjust to academic demands?
2. What is a reasonable amount of time to spend with a student who needs special assistance? What is an unreasonable amount of time?
3. Was Jack wrong to schedule the first before-class tutoring session? Could Jack have known during that first conversation with Pam that this session would become a regular part of the class?
4. Was Jack justified in trying to curtail the conferences with Pam? If so, how could he have curtailed them without alienating a fragile student?
5. To what extent was Jack responsible for helping Pam get over her writing "problems" and her fear of university classes?

Seeing Strengths and Weaknesses

James O'Laughlin

The spring semester course Intermediate Composition was unusually small — only seven students rather than the usual 15 to 20. During the first class meeting, the instructor, Michael, asked the students to tell the class a little about themselves and their previous writing experiences. Going around the room, each student stood up, said where he or she was from, gave some information about his or her educational background and occupation, and talked about his or her writing. Ralph appeared disinterested during this introductory exercise, and when it was his turn to speak, he said little.

Nonetheless, after class was dismissed, Ralph stayed. Pointing at the syllabus, he asked Michael, "Why should I be asked to write about the assigned readings for the papers in this course instead of being able to write about things I know I am interested in? After all, this is a writing course, not a course in political philosophy or social theory. Plus, some of these essays you have us writing about have to do with theories that I think are wrong."

"Have you read these essays before?" Michael asked somewhat rhetorically.

Ralph stared at him in response.

Michael tried to explain that he would have plenty of flexibility in the assignments to develop his own analysis and use the essays in a creative way as models of thinking about the subject matter.

Ralph remained silent.

Not knowing what else to do, Michael excused himself and left the classroom.

The next two classes went quite well, Michael thought, except with regard to Ralph. While the other students had discussed at length a series of questions about the readings Michael had carefully scripted, Ralph just rolled his eyes.

The only time he spoke was at the end of class to note that one of the writers had a basic misunderstanding about his subject matter. Ralph didn't provide support for his comment, and, since it was 9:00 P.M. and Michael had a business trip the next morning, he did not ask him to elaborate.

The papers Michael received the next week were impressive overall. While they contained some mechanical problems, the students seemed to have done well with the assignment, which was to critically analyze two of the articles that had been discussed during the previous class session. But Ralph's paper was not on par with his classmates' work. He had strayed from the assignment substantially. Michael had provided his students with a number of options for the paper, which he outlined in the syllabus. Yet, Ralph had done something only tangentially related to any of those options.

At the end of his comments on the paper, Michael asked Ralph to see him after class. Throughout the following class period, while his six classmates eagerly engaged in the discussion, Ralph said nothing. He fiddled with his paper a few times, looking at some of Michael's notes in the margins and then ducked out as soon as the class period was over without ever speaking to Michael.

During the next two class sessions, Ralph participated more frequently, but in Michael's opinion, his comments about the readings generally dismissed out of hand both the essayists' own arguments and the other class members' comments. At times he sounded as if he were giving a monologue.

"All of the essays we've read in here have missed the basic point about people's problems," Ralph said.

"They all see society as at least partly to blame for an individual's problems. That's wrong. What everyone needs to do is realize that only they can solve their own problems by a change of attitude." Ralph went on to cite what Michael considered "New Age" philosophy books as support for his position.

The other students appeared bored and said nothing to

rebut Ralph's comments, or even to inquire into them, despite Michael's efforts to get them going.

On the next paper, Ralph stayed within the boundaries of the assignment, but Michael still felt he ignored the key objective of the assignment, which was to illustrate both the strengths and weaknesses of holding any given assumption. The students were instructed to use one or two of the assigned readings for examples to support their positions. Ralph did talk about two of the assigned essays in his paper, but he did not critique them as the assignment required — he failed to include any strengths or positive implications relating to the authors' arguments. Instead, he simply rehashed the point he had made in class about how the authors were wrong and how people just need to change their attitudes; then he mentioned some more New-Age thinkers.

When Michael had encountered this type of resistance to critical thinking in composition classes before, he used the comments on the papers and individual conferences to help guide the students past it. Ralph, however, had already rebuffed his attempt to have a conference on his first paper, and he had voiced objections from the beginning about reading material outside of his areas of interest. From his second paper and his comments in class, it seemed to Michael that Ralph simply had no interest in writing the kind of paper that had been assigned.

A more serious problem was that the other students seemed to be retreating. They became more reticent when Ralph dismissed the readings in class. Michael felt that this type of rejection was counterproductive and created a potential stumbling block to the other students' fully appreciating the level of critical analysis he was looking for in their papers. Ralph's behavior was also undercutting the approach Michael wanted his students to take toward each others' writing in the classroom — pointing out both the strengths and the weaknesses, not merely one or the other, and especially not just focusing on the weaknesses, which he knew nearly all writers tended to take personally.

****

Michael writes position papers in the Chicago office of a social policy Washington-based think tank. He prefers living in Chicago because his parents and siblings live in the area and his children are in grade school in a local parochial school. But his job requires long hours and frequent trips to Washington, DC, sometimes as often as six times a month.

Despite his professional demands, he enjoys the challenges of teaching. He especially enjoys the wide range of experiences and ways of thinking that adult students at the college invariably bring to the classroom. Yet this is the first time he has taught this particular course, having taught the introductory composition class for the past three years.

Michael believes that critical analysis is crucial to effective writing. To help his students develop their critical thinking skills, he carefully selects essays on controversial topics that are of common knowledge, usually articles he has run across in his work. For the intermediate course he selected some fairly difficult essays, which he planned to discuss in class.

Michael's approach involves heavy classroom discussion. As far as he is concerned, that is one of the best ways to encourage his students to think critically. He tries to engage the students to talk about more than the organization, sentence structure, and style of the required readings, to get them to evaluate the substance of the authors' arguments.

In his previous classes, he had found that the students thrived on the discussion format he used. They would draw on examples from their personal experience and find ways, as the course progressed, to integrate and assess the limits of each others' viewpoints. In his opinion, the rapport among the students in class was a necessary ingredient to the success of that classroom dynamic. They might not like each other, but they would take each others' positions and comments seriously. Michael found that his discussion and workshop format had always generated lively debate with a fair amount of disagreement.

However, there were one or two students who did not get into the flow of discussion on a regular basis. This always irritated Michael a little bit. Nonetheless, he usually found ways of connecting with those students in individual conferences and monitoring their progress more closely in that way, and class discussions did not seem to suffer appreciably from one or two students' reticence.

******

Ralph is a thirty-one-year-old computer salesman who is searching for a new direction in life. He has been feeling as if he is plodding along in his career, not really enjoying his job but not hating it either. He always loved writing and decided to take classes at the university.

Prior to this course, he was six hours shy of a thirty-hour writing certificate with an emphasis in non-fiction writing, which is his goal. He hopes to ultimately write free-lance articles about his area of interest — contemporary philosophy and religion. He spent the vast majority of his time outside of work and class reading New Age philosophies, Eastern religious scholars, and self-help books and articles. He had begged his advisor to let him do an independent study writing a couple of longer pieces exploring one or two specific theories of his choosing, but his advisor told him that would not satisfy any course requirements, so he grudgingly signed up for Intermediate Composition.

****

The next week Ralph's second paper was scheduled for class discussion. Michael considered telling him that he wanted to wait and exhibit a later paper because this one only repeated what he thought were the more regrettable aspects of his contributions about New Age philosophy to the class discussion from the previous week. But he decided that waiting might make matters worse or, at best, simply postpone the issue.

After discussing two other papers, about which Ralph

offered only criticism, the class read Ralph's paper. One of Michael's rules of discussion was that the author could not speak during a critique of his or his paper, but would be permitted to comment at the end of the discussion. When Michael asked the other students for their impressions of Ralph's work, no one spoke.

"Do you think the author of this paper fully discussed both the strengths and the weaknesses of the arguments in the two essays that he analyzed?" he asked the class, hoping that by rephrasing his question he could encourage someone to comment.

Still silence.

Michael's face got red and he felt the back of his neck get warm. He was becoming very angry with Ralph. Michael felt Ralph had cowed the class into silence. "The weaknesses in his approach are obvious," Michael thought. "The other students must know, but they're not willing to challenge him."

Michael tried one more tactic to get the class to discuss Ralph's paper. He read a passage from his paper that he thought was most representative of the weaknesses in his analysis. The passage summarized the basic position of one of the required readings — a scholarly interpretation of the Clarence Thomas–Anita Hill Senate confirmation hearings in relation to theories of the public sphere. After his summary, Ralph's next paragraph contained only one word: "Really." In Michael's opinion, the following paragraphs, which included a discussion of the "New Age" correctives Ralph had raised in class, did not elaborate on his one-word rejection of the author's argument. Moreover, he felt the passage completely ignored any real appreciation of the essay's strong points.

"Do you think that someone can provide a full critical analysis of the essay by using one word such as 'really'?" Michael asked the class.

The class sat silent for a moment fidgeting in their seats. Michael was about to try one more exasperated attempt to get someone to say something about Ralph's paper when finally one student spoke up.

"It kind of makes you wonder why the student bothered to write about this essay, or even why they are taking the class."

"It makes me wonder too," Ralph said, and he collected his belongings and walked out.

Questions:

1. What should Michael do now? Should he call Ralph before the next class, so he doesn't drop the course? What could he say to him?
2. During the remainder of the class period, how should he handle his departure or the events that transpired that night? Or should he say nothing?
3. What other ways of dealing with Ralph's paper could Michael have tried?
4. Should Michael have tried harder to have a conference with Ralph before his second paper?
5. To what extent should an instructor give extra leeway to a student such as Ralph, especially given his initial concerns about the required reading?
6. Should an instructor accept that there will always be one or two "dissatisfied customers" in a class, regardless of the size of the class? If yes, then what do you do to avoid putting off the rest of the students, especially when it is a small class? If no, how do you please these students without losing sight of your primary goal at the risk of losing the interest of the rest of the class?

A Brief Course in Conflict
Andra Medea

Part I

For the past several years, Erica Johnsen had taught a course on interpersonal conflict in the continuing education division at a major university. Because the course addressed issues in work and family life and encouraged students to draw on their own experiences, it got strong responses from adult learners.

There were often thirty or forty students in her class, large relative to other evening courses. So many students sometimes led to conditions a shade short of crowd control. Still, the interactive nature of the class gave it its power and vitality.

Given the limits of discussion in a large group, most students were cooperative, were appropriately restrained, and held themselves to high intellectual standards. Except for Jane. There was nothing "ivory tower" about Jane. She was blunt and unmistakably honest, but so devoid of social skills that it was nearly impossible to work with her. There was no telling when Jane would disrupt the class with sudden tirades or outbursts.

Early in the semester, the class was discussing alliances and the intricate shifts in balance that could take place under pressure. The discussion was spirited; a number of students made insightful comments on their work and families. Then Jane raised her hand and said, "I just want to know why is it people have to act so f—ing stupid? I mean, why do they have to act so stupid? I just need to know this."

Erica was nonplussed. She had hit her stride during the class debate, but at this, her jaw dropped. She tried to think how this could be related to anything that had been said previously in the discussion. Erica finally said, "I take it you have something on your mind. What is it you're trying to say?"

Jane repeated her statement several times, then said, "I keep trying to get a meeting about this screw-up that's happened over my transcript. I've notified my advisor, the entire academic staff, the financial aid department, and the dean of the college. I'm trying to get them to all sit down, and all I get is the runaround."

Not sure at all that she should be pursuing this in class, Erica nevertheless ventured, "Why would the dean of the college need to meet with you about your transcript?"

"Because everyone's screwed up, and it's time they know about it!"

Erica decided that this was as far as they needed to discuss this topic in class. She tried to return to the original topic, but she couldn't regain her train of thought. She finally shifted to another subject.

Similar episodes happened in every subsequent class meeting. While other students would explore ideas and experiment with conflict management techniques, Jane would go into tirades, after which the rest of the students would go dead silent. Erica was reminded of how people edge away from a person standing on a street corner yelling obscenities.

Jane's papers were more of the same. In response to an assignment to write a five-page paper, Jane turned in a twelve-page, single-spaced tirade that did not mention the assigned topic. It was a well-organized tirade, with bullet points and good grammar, but it had nothing whatsoever to do with the assignment.

I shouldn't let this get to me, Erica would tell herself. However, it was getting to her, and she was afraid it was starting to show. Each week she would walk into class and hope that Jane would not be there. Unfortunately, she always was. Other students began to miss class. Those in class appeared frustrated and distracted, and classroom discussion grew strained. Eventually, Erica dreaded even walking in the door. I am a professional, she would tell herself. I'm a professional in conflict management and a professional teacher and I can handle this. A throbbing headache would start two hours before class and last well into the next day. Erica got so upset by Jane that she could barely pay attention to the other students.

Erica tried to think of how other teachers she had known would have dealt with such an extreme problem. One of her professors had handled personality conflicts by disposing of the offending students. He would take them aside and say, "I strongly suggest you drop this class, because there is no way under heaven that you are going to pass this course." Erica knew something was wrong when brute force began to look appealing.

Contemplating the situation, Erica realized that Jane's outlandish behavior bore a resemblance to other situations she had seen in classrooms and other walks of life: opinionated people, people who dominated discussions, people who constantly griped, people who brought their family dilemmas to school or the workplace, people who would not follow directions. Yet the extreme nature of Jane's behavior seemed to put her in a category all her own.

The problem came to a head during a role play of a problem-solving technique. Erica needed someone to be an angry customer. Jane volunteered. No one else moved a muscle. Erica thought, I'm sure I can deal with this.

Jane immediately launched into a diatribe that had nothing to do with the role play. "You don't care about me. You don't care about what's going wrong with me. Nobody cares about anything around here. Financial aid could flush my files down the toilet and you wouldn't care a thing about it!"

Erica felt her face flush with anger. She felt betrayed and blindsided. Her sense of fair play felt violated; her privacy felt violated; her role as a professional in charge of this class felt violated. Yet she could not allow herself to lose her temper and let this student disrupt everything.

Erica gave up the role play as a dead loss. She said, as calmly as she could, "I understand that you're upset, but this class has twenty-four other students, and I have material I need to cover. I will sit down with you after class and discuss this but I am not going to sidetrack class and discuss this here and now."

To Erica's surprise, Jane calmed down immediately. She said that meeting after class was a good idea and returned to her seat without another word. As though the exchange were a legitimate role play, the class calmly dissected Erica and Jane's encounter. To Erica's embarrassment, the class's assessment was that Erica had come very close to losing it. Her pride hurting, Erica limped through the remainder of class.

When the other students had left, she sat down with Jane. Early in their conversation, Erica realized that Jane came from an enormously dysfunctional family. She may not have many social skills, but based on what Jane told her, she seemed far ahead of her relations.

Erica voiced her concern that Jane did not appear to be learning anything in this class. Jane's outbursts at the beginning of the semester were unchanged from her outbursts later in the semester. Few of the skills seemed to be filtering though. Perhaps Jane should think about dropping the course, although only four weeks remained in the fourteen-week semester.

The next morning, Erica's head still ached from her encounter with Jane. She decided to check with Jane's advisor to make sure the recommendation to drop the class made it onto some official record.

Jane's advisor was equally exasperated. True, Jane was hard working, and her writing and research were, at least technically, up to par. However, her behavior was so inappropriate it was hard for her to function at the university. She currently had separate feuds running with financial aid, the administration, the dean of the college, and the provost of the university. The advisor had also heard some background about Jane's family. Although Jane seems the most functional person the family had yet produced, she was driving everyone crazy. Because of her temper, she would probably be just as unemployable after receiving her degree as she was without it.

Erica told the advisor that she would have to flunk Jane if she didn't bring in her work and show signs of having absorbed material from class.

Arriving at class the next week, Erica expected Jane to have dropped the course. Instead, Jane arrived with a stack of papers, which she placed on Erica's desk. They were rewrites of her past papers as well as one paper she had not submitted. Jane was relatively quiet during the class period.

The day after that class meeting, Erica began reading Jane's papers and was surprised to find them quite acceptable. While they didn't show a sophisticated use of conflict-management techniques, they did show that Jane could use the techniques—and in overwhelmingly difficult situations. In one case, Jane wrote about handling a brawl between her screaming mother, who suffered from Alzheimer's disease, and Jane's sister, who was abusive and at that time staggering drunk. Erica thought, Jane isn't doing badly, considering the magnitude of the conflicts she faces.

Erica returned the papers to Jane with her comments and without any mention of dropping the class. The final paper was due the next week. Erica hoped that Jane would continue to hold her temper and hand in a decent final paper; then the semester, mercifully, would be over.

When the last class arrived, Jane turned in her paper with the rest of the students. Erica felt relieved. Yet her anxiety returned when she read the paper the next day. It was a full regression to her earlier work: a well-written tirade that did not address the assignment.

Questions:
1. What can an instructor do when a student is obviously unsuited—whether by temperament or skill—for a university class?
2. How should an instructor cope with a student who is aca-

demically capable, but emotionally troubled? Does an instructor have any role in helping an emotionally troubled student?

3. How can an instructor intervene when a student disrupts the class?

4. In what ways might the instructor in this case have dealt with Jane earlier?

5. Were any of the instructor's attempts to solve this prob lem effective?

6. Given the current situation—satisfactory work handed in late and an unsatisfactory final paper—what should the instructor do now?

7. Erica observes that Jane's behavior is an extreme version of some more common characteristics that other students may have. Would any of the techniques an instructor might use to cope with, for example, a student who domi- nated discussions apply to the situation with Jane?

Part II

Erica felt she had no choice. She gave Jane an F on the paper, which meant she failed the course. Erica returned the paper to Jane in the stamped, self-addressed envelope that all the students provided, and she told herself, without any satisfaction, that finally the semester was over.

Several days later, Erica's telephone at home rang. Jane was distressed. She couldn't understand what she was sup- posed to do. As Jane and Erica talked, Erica found herself thinking that Jane did not understand the very concept of dealing effectively with conflict. Her writing skills were fine, as were her research skills. But real-life problem-solving, a basic component of the course, threw her into a panic.

If Jane lacked the concept of effective conflict manage- ment, Erica realized, she couldn't very well write a paper about it. With this thought in mind, Erica asked Jane, "Was there some time when you were in a situation full of con- flict, but you used one of the techniques we discussed in class and things got better?"

Surprisingly, Jane did have an instance—a remarkably

moving one that resulted in reconciliation with her brother. But, she told Erica, she didn't think that event counted. After all, she had effectively resolved the conflict so the problem must not have been so bad after all.

Erica and Jane then negotiated an arrangement under which Jane would turn in a new paper analyzing the resolution she reached with her brother. Jane turned in the paper, which, after one rewrite proved satisfactory.

As Erica filled out the change-of-grade report, she was still far from satisfied with how the semester had turned out. She was going to pass Jane, but she wished she could use a special grade: CX, meaning, This is a C, but don't ever sign up for one of my classes again!

Questions:
1. Should Erica have failed Jane after reading her final paper? What alternatives did she have?
2. When Jane called, upset about the grade, should Erica have given her the chance to rewrite the paper?
3. Was the outcome of Erica and Jane's work during the semester—and especially on the last paper—desirable? Was it worth the effort? Might an equally good or better outcome have been achieved with less struggle?

Part III:
Cases from a Student Perspective

Confronting the Grade
Lydia Rohn

Setting

This case takes place in the continuing education school of a large Midwestern university. The students, whose ages range from approximately twenty-five to sixty-five, pursue diverse goals. Some are seeking degrees or certificates necessary to change careers or advance in current careers, while others simply enjoy learning and are less concerned with earning credits. Most instructors are employed outside the university and teach one or two courses per semester. Most classes meet one evening per week.

The Problem

Mary had been looking forward to this class meeting all week. She had been enjoying the course—Marketing Methods—and was confident she had correctly answered each question on last week's first of two exams. She could visualize the "A" written on the cover of her blue exam booklet. However, Mary was held up in traffic on the way to class and arrived a bit late. As she entered the classroom, the instructor, Allison Carne, looked up, smiled, and held Mary's bluebook out toward her. Mary took the booklet, holding it face-side down, and started toward a seat in the back, listening as Ms. Carne discussed the first question from the exam.

Mary purposely did not look at her grade, wanting to heighten the suspense before she saw her "A." After she had deposited her purse on the back of the seat and her books on the desktop, she turned over her bluebook. On the cover, in red ink, was written "85%." Mary flinched and looked up. On the board was a grading scale. Mary quickly scanned it and found that 85 percent corresponded to a "C."

Mary's heart thumped as she quickly flipped through the booklet, looking for answers with points deducted. She interrupted her search to look around the room for any other dismayed faces and did see one other student—a woman about Mary's age—who seemed shaken.

Although distracted by her disappointment, Mary tried to listen to the discussion about the exam and was surprised to hear that Ms. Carne's explanations seemed to match the answers Mary had written in her bluebook. Jaw tight, Mary joined in the discussion. She purposely gave an answer from which Ms. Carne had deducted five points and was astonished to hear her respond, "That's right, Mary."

As the evening's lecture began, Mary found her attention stuck on the exam. Perhaps, she thought, she was being petty. After all, 85 percent was not a terrible mark. But how could an 85 percent equal a "C," and what would that do to her final grade for the semester? What grades had others in the class received? Maybe an 85 percent was a high score compared with the others.

Mary told herself that she was making too much of her grade. She thought, I should be concerned with what I learn, not what grade I get. But grades are important to me, especially this grade—I studied hours and hours for this exam. Besides, if I got a "C," then Ms. Carne is not a very good instructor. If I'm misunderstanding that much of the material, I'll bet everyone else is, too. But apparently I'm not missing the material; Ms. Carne just told me my "wrong" answer was actually right. This isn't fair.

The more Mary thought about her grade, the angrier she became. She wondered if she should speak to Ms. Carne during break. One thing was for sure: she wanted to talk to the other students in the class as soon as possible to find out their reactions to the exam.

Finally, Ms. Carne paused in her lecture to say, "Let's take a fifteen minute break," and Mary headed straight for Karen, her best friend in class.

"So, Karen, did you do OK?"

Karen said, breathlessly, "Can you believe it? I got an 'A.' I guess I understood this subject better than I thought.

Thanks for all your help with my studying. How did you do?"

"I got a 'C', and I'm furious. I can't believe she marked some of my answers wrong. When I gave the same answers just now in class she said they were right. I'm thinking about talking to her. This isn't fair." Mary noticed that Karen was looking sheepish. "What is it?"

Karen told her that she had noticed during the discussion that some of her answers were different from what had been said just now in class. "Mary, I know that two of my answers were clearly wrong, but Ms. Carne gave me full credit for both. Now when I hear what happened to you I know I have to tell her."

"No!" Mary said. "You need all the points you can get out of this class. Just leave it alone."

They discussed whether Mary should confront Ms. Carne about the grade. Mary was worried that if she spoke up, Ms. Carne would think she was attacking her. Maybe she would get angry and lower the grade even further or give her a bad grade on the final exam out of spite. Karen said that Mary had to talk to Ms. Carne, that even if Ms. Carne got upset, Mary would know that she was doing the right thing.

As Mary and Karen returned from break, Mary saw that the student who had seemed upset during the discussion in class was now in an earnest conversation with Ms. Carne at her desk. As Mary passed, she heard Ms. Carne saying, "We can talk about this more another time."

During the remainder of the class period, Mary could pay no attention to the lecture. She knew that she had to confront Ms. Carne after class, and she wondered how she could do that without any bad repercussions. As the lecture continued, Mary rehearsed what she would say to Ms. Carne.

About Mary

Mary had been a highly motivated employee who had excelled and advanced quickly through her professional career. She recently had suspended her career to stay home with her three small children and return to school to complete a bachelor of science degree related to her career. She chose this university because of its prestigious reputation and its acceptance of sixty hours of prior course work at both a state college and a junior college. Mary also was a very motivated student and devoted many hours studying to excel in each course she undertook. In ten courses at this university, Mary had maintained a near-perfect grade point average. Mary also enjoyed the camaraderie in this continuing education program. For example, she spent many hours with her fellow student, Karen, helping her study and reassuring her that she would do well in the classes they took together.

About Ms. Carne

Like many of the instructors in this continuing education program, Allison Carne worked full-time outside of the university and taught part-time in the evenings. For five years, she had been teaching Marketing Methods as well as one other business course. Often, her lectures included her own professional experiences, providing examples that helped the students understand the theories taught in the course. Her students seemed to enjoy this aspect of her teaching.

At the beginning of this course, Ms. Carne conveyed to her students her disappointment with the textbook she had assigned, but said she had yet to find a better one. She discussed the syllabus, providing basic information about how the class would proceed. The syllabus outlined the topics to be covered in each class period. In addition, the syllabus noted that the course would include three exams, one a final exam covering the entire course. The syllabus also stated that a paper would be required, but did not state the due date or any details about form or content. The syllabus did not specifically describe the teaching technique or the evaluation method. Ms. Carne assumed that adult students would not need such "hand-holding"; her experience was that they would expect a combination of lecture and discussion and would study hard without concern for how grades were determined. However, during the introductory discussion, she did advise the students to concentrate on the lectures and on the "main ideas" in the textbook, but not to emphasize its outdated examples.

When the first exam was approaching, Ms. Carne told the class that it would consist of ten short-answer essay questions worth ten points each. She advised students to write answers that were "short and to the point," that she tended to give higher scores to answers that were both correct and concise.

She had never encountered a conflict with a student about a grade or any other aspect of her courses, although she had noted a smattering of mild concerns about her grading in the student evaluations she received at the end of each semester. She assumed that all instructors received a few such comments.

Discussion

After the class ended, Mary hung back until all the other students had left. Karen paused at the door, looked back, and gave Mary a wink.

Mary approached the front desk, where Ms. Carne was putting papers into her briefcase. She waited for Ms. Carne to look up, then said in a joking tone, "I have to tell you that your exams scare me to death!"

"Why is that? You didn't do so badly."

"Well, when I left class last week, I was sure I had aced the exam. Then, this week, when I got the exam back I was shocked. I was so upset that I could barely listen to the lecture tonight."

Ms. Carne nodded, but did not comment.

Mary continued, "Do you think we could discuss the questions I missed?"

"Okay," said Ms. Carne, sitting. "But as I recall, you didn't really 'miss' any of the questions. Let's see what you wrote and I'll tell you what I was looking for."

Mary, leaning over the desk, set her bluebook down in from of Ms. Carne and opened it to the first question with points deducted. As Ms. Carne looked on, Mary recited the question, read her answer, and explained why she believed the answer was correct. She was surprised that she was able to express herself so clearly, considering that her heart was thumping hard. She had never been this nervous when having a disagreement in a business situation. She felt like she had less power, less control here.

"You're right," said Ms. Carne. "You should have gotten more points for that answer." She took a pen from her briefcase, uncapped it, drew a line through the "-3 " in the margin, and wrote "OK" underneath. She looked up at Mary, smiled apologetically, and said, "I graded these while I was away on business—while I was on an airplane, as a matter of fact. Maybe I was working too quickly."

Mary nodded, concealing her surprise at what seemed a thin excuse. She quickly turned to another page in the book, again recited the question, and pointed out the key elements of her answer. "Why is this wrong?" Mary asked, and immediately regretted what seemed a challenging tone.

Ms. Carne asked her to explain her answer in more detail, and Mary obliged. Ms. Carne nodded and said, "You know the subject well, but why didn't you include what you just said in your answer?"

"Well...I...you said to keep the answers concise, to the point. That's what I was trying to do." She felt her voice rising in pitch. "How am I supposed to know which details you want us to include in our 'concise' answers? Besides, you only covered these details casually in class. You gave no clue these were so important that they should be part of our answers."

Ms. Carne took a deep breath. "Mary, tell me something. You've taken many classes in the evening program here. How do the other instructors structure their exams? How do they grade?"

Mary said that she had always done well on other exams, that if she showed she understood the concept, she got full credit. "Also," she said, "on other exams, the questions are more specific than yours, so it's easier to know what information we're expected to give. The questions here seem too general for us to know what answer you're looking for." Inwardly, Mary winced. She told herself to stay calm—to avoid turning this into a confrontation.

Ms. Carne took another deep breath. "Okay, fine. I'll give you this one, too. Perhaps you simply have trouble summarizing your ideas."

Mary wanted to protest, but stopped herself. Just let me get through this, she thought. As she turned the booklet to the next page, she noticed that the student who had been talking with Ms. Carne at break had returned and was standing in the doorway. Mary felt awkward having this audience, but kept her voice low and pushed on, restating the next question and her answer.

In the middle of Mary's attempt to explain why her answer was correct, Ms. Carne interrupted. "Enough, already. You can have this one too. You've got your 'A.'" She glanced toward the student in the doorway and grimaced.

Mary mumbled a "thanks" but immediately regretted that obsequiousness. She quickly gathered her papers, then edged past the waiting student and out the door. Walking toward her car, she felt her stomach churn. She had gotten what she had wanted out of the discussion with Ms. Carne— a better grade, the grade she felt she deserved. But the feeling that the discussion had gone terribly wrong gnawed at her.

The Sequel
    Mary contributed infrequently to class discussions during the remainder of the semester. When it came time to study for the next exam, she found herself unsure how to proceed and bitter that she should have to take a test with such ambiguous expectations. She gave more detail than a "concise" answer would normally have and was the last student to

complete the exam. She received a 92 percent, which Ms. Carne equated with a "B+." Mary received another B+ on her paper, with the comment, "Good job," written across the top, but no other detail.

When time came for the final exam, Mary felt at a loss. She studied copiously and wrote even more extensive answers than she had written on the previous exam. Again, she was the last student to complete the exam, which she placed on Ms. Carne's desk without meeting the instructor's eyes.

While she waited to receive her final grade in the mail, Mary continued to think about the class: How could Ms. Carne have been so unfair? What was a student supposed to do in a situation like this?

Questions:
1. How could Mary have better handled the discussion with Ms. Carne? Did she cover the necessary issues? Did she achieve her goals for the discussion? Should she have enlisted Karen's assistance?
2. What other options did Mary have for trying to change the way grades were given in this class?
3. Was Mary overly concerned with grades? What elements in Mary's background may have contributed to this situation?
4. Based on the information given, was Ms. Carne's exam unfair? Isn't all grading to some degree subjective, especially grading of essay exams?
5. What could Ms. Carne do to improve her handling of exams and grades? What kind of approach might convince her to change her practice? What in her background may have contributed to this situation?
6. Should students expect that, inevitably, they will have a few instructors who are "difficult" or possibly unfair graders and simply accept that situation?
7. Is confronting an instructor about a grade worthwhile? Do instructors have the last word about a grade? If no, is Mary's situation bad enough to warrant a complaint to a dean?

A Case of Diffidence
Leslie Fischer

On the first night of his English Composition II course, Robert Holmes addressed the class, "I believe it's important to be sure you can stand before you attempt to walk; you must float before you attempt to swim. Consequently, we won't do much writing until I'm sure you can manage the elements of grammar, so in the last hour of class you will complete a diagnostic grammar examination." The class groaned. An experienced teacher, Robert good-humoredly continued, "Now don't worry; this is simply diagnostic, so it won't count toward your grade. However, at the end of the term you will take a grammar exam that will count. I think you'll be amazed by your improvement at the end of the semester."

He continued outlining the course and its objectives. Jean Greenwood was relieved to see that the assignments became less prescriptive as the term progressed. Just before break, Robert asked his students to describe the courses they had taken and their professions. Jean answered briefly, "English and Chemistry. Assistant Curator at the Regina Museum." Robert responded, "Good, I can at least expect some logic and method in your writing."

With trepidation, Jean had enrolled for her second term English Composition II course. Ms. Phillips, Jean's instructor from the fall-term course, Introduction to English Composition, had tried to prepare her, "Mr. Holmes' class will be quite different from mine. He's more detail-oriented and is likely to be very exacting on elements such as grammar and structure, as well as content. I think you're up to it."

Jean wasn't so sure. She recalled her decision to register for Ms. Phillips' class. She was brushing her hair that morning head down, when she decided. As she righted herself, she grimaced in the mirror. "What doesn't kill me makes me stronger," she growled in her best movie tough guy imitation. She felt like that now, but she knew better than to say it to Ms. Phillips.

She had been pleasantly surprised by the warm and nurturing atmosphere of Ms. Phillips' classroom. The writing process had been broken into such small steps that the students hardly realized how far they had progressed until the last night of class when they compared their early work with the final paper of the term. Jean's grammar and organization had improved considerably; even more important to Jean, her style had strengthened and grown into an engaging, playful, yet incisive writer's voice. Jean was pleased.

She knew many students claimed to suffer from writer's block, but she had difficulty imagining a case worse than hers. A naturally shy and rather diffident child, Jean felt her grammar school education had done little to encourage her to speak or to write what she really thought. She had no trouble generating ideas, but her thoughts were so quirky that, having more than once received a dismayed look from her teachers, she usually kept all but her most obvious ideas to herself. Of course, this strategy encouraged her daydreaming and one day, while absently chewing a scrap of notebook paper, she was startled by her math teacher's booming baritone, "Greenwood, what are you doing?"

"Nothing, sir." As soon as she said it, Jean knew it was the wrong answer.

"It looks like you're chewing that paper."

Jean had nothing to add to his observation, so she concentrated on the wood grain patterns of her desk.

"You like the taste of paper, Greenwood?"

Jean thought, "No, I like the feel of it," but knew that was the wrong answer. Mutely, she stared harder at her desk.

"Here, eat this," and with that Mr. Watson balled up a sheet of her notebook paper and stuffed it in her mouth.

Throughout the rest of grammar school and high school, Jean communicated little because she knew that whatever she said or wrote would be wrong. The college prep curriculum was not for her; she concentrated her efforts in Home

Economics, where she simply followed recipes or dress pattern instructions, so she couldn't go too far wrong; as she gained confidence, she even introduced her own variations. Her diligence and creativity endeared her to her teacher, who found her a job in a weaving studio upon graduation. Jean had never woven so much as a potholder, but she became fascinated with the possibilities of fibers and weave structures. An industrious if quiet employee, Jean took on increasing responsibilities that brought her work to the attention of one of the board members of the fledgling textile museum. In her new position, Jean learned to conserve and restore textiles, picking up a not insignificant amount of chemistry along the way.

She had worked her way up to assistant curator when the director of the museum suggested Jean would need further education if she hoped to advance professionally. With what Jean saw as a great deal of courage she signed up for chemistry and English composition in the adult education division of a prestigious private university that offered a program in Museum Conservancy. If she had to drop the English course, she reasoned, at least she'd have the chemistry.

On the first night of English class, Jean discovered that Ms. Phillips possessed an amateur's love of textiles. There was much that Jean could teach her through essays that often employed textile themes or imagery. Jean enjoyed the novel feeling of educating her teacher; Ms. Phillips seemed genuinely interested in what she had to say. Robert Holmes was different.

Not only did he seem disinterested in what she had to say, he seemed to insist that she write her uninteresting thoughts in his way. In the third week of the term, Jean reviewed her English assignment: Write a four-to-five sentence paragraph summarizing Stephen Hawking's "The Uncertainty Principle" from *A Brief History of Time*. Your paragraph should point out the salient features of Hawking's position, briefly characterizing his major points. You should also include a thesis sentence that summarizes the entire paragraph. Remember, do not inject your own point of view. Be completely objective.

Jean thought back to the class discussion. Hadn't Mr. Holmes summarized the chapter on the board, outlining four or five points? She checked her notes — yes, there it was, just like the instructions on a dress pattern — first this, then that with the result a finished paragraph made to Holmes' order. Why would he ask us to regurgitate this, Jean wondered. It seemed to be what Holmes wanted. Her guess was borne out when her summary was returned to her with an A-.

Subsequent guesses as to Robert Holmes' expectations were not quite so successful. In fact as the term progressed, Jean's grades steadily declined. By midterm conferences, Jean was receiving Cs. Highly concerned about her deteriorating performance, Robert thought back over her class participation. She was such a quiet student, one of those with whom he couldn't think of any conversation beyond a simple hello and comments about the weather, though she seemed to have plenty to say to her classmates. He recalled walking back into the classroom during a break. Jean was quietly talking to a group of six or seven students, so quietly he couldn't hear what she said, although her classmates were quite silent in their strained attention to catch her story. She stopped speaking, and for fully five seconds there was silence—then a sudden burst of laughter from her listeners. Throughout the rest of class that evening, he could do little to stimulate discussion. Most of the students he thought of as the "old reliables" in class participation had been among Jean's audience, but that night they wore rather bemused smiles and remained silent.

Jean would never have been considered one of the old reliables; he had to make a conscious effort to call on her to encourage her participation. She always answered inquiries quite competently; one or two of her comments had surprisingly challenged ideas that he had held dear for a very long time. He was careful not to let on; it was important that his students rely on his authority.

Convinced of Jean's keen intelligence, Robert thought of ways to encourage her to take more risks in her writing. Jean seemed uncomfortable expressing herself. Robert suspected that she was a writer more comfortable with hard and fast rules, with structures more formal than the rather intuitive and creative direction toward which he had been trying to move his students. After all, he thought, hers is a scientific mind; we need to inject some creativity into it.

"Well Jean, you started the term very strongly, but you seem to be meeting some problems with your writing right now." Robert watched her trace the paisley pattern of her notebook with her finger. She looked scared, and Robert wondered how to encourage her.

Robert maintained his voice at its normal pitch, but with a cheery quality he hoped would encourage Jean to speak up. "You need to learn to trust your intuition. Now that you have more freedom to write what you want, you have to learn to develop some independence. You need to experiment with which guidelines you'll follow and which you'll reject. I want you to use your own judgment."

His tone of voice seemed to work, for Jean responded more strongly, "I don't understand. You mean you want us to go against what you've taught?"

"Not necessarily..." he began.

Jean seemed agitated; the pitch of her voice rose. "I was using my own judgment to begin with, but you said we had to follow your rules."

Robert tried to diffuse her agitation with a light tone. He laughed. "Rules were made to be broken." The look on Jean's face sobered him. "I just wanted to give you a strong foundation, so you could make informed decisions about your writing. You have a background in science, surely you can understand the logic of that?"

Jean glanced at him then down at her notebook. Her voice became quiet. "I'm sorry, I'm just not cut out for college writing. I must be stupid; I just can't see the consistency behind your method. You seem to be switching expectations in midstream. I have tried to follow your advice, but you didn't seem interested in what I had to say, just whether I was saying it in your way."

Annoyed, Robert said in an exasperated tone, "That's unfair, I'm trying to give you the benefit of my experience."

Jean bit her lip, "I'm sorry, I should go."

Jean raged at both Robert's methods and her own diffidence all the way to her apartment, but assuaged her anger when she reached the haven of home with her traditional remedy of soaking her feet in hot, scented water and sipping herbal tea. *I'm so stupid for not writing as I wanted from the beginning, but he's just like Mr. Watson,* she thought angrily. The soak and the tea began to do their work. *No, that's not fair; he's intelligent. He's got a lot of teaching experience, but I just can't do this his way. I can't write, now that he's given me so many rules to accept or reject before I'm allowed to convey my ideas. His teaching works for others, but it just doesn't work for me. At least I still have Chem. II. I should call Mr. Holmes and let him know I need to drop the class.*

"I've got my own issues to deal with; it's not your fault, you just remind me of a teacher I had problems with in grammar school." As he played Jean's message on his answering machine, Robert felt insulted. *I've done absolutely nothing to deserve comparison with a ghost from her past,* he thought, *except to provide the foundations that woman needs to become a good writer.* He shrugged and sighed to himself. *Well, I guess some students just have a lot of baggage they bring into the classroom; there's not much I can do to help them.*

Questions:
1. How might the professor and the student have communicated more fully earlier in the semester?
2. To what extent is a student responsible for communicat-

ing questions or apprehensions about class design to an instructor?

3. To what extent is an instructor responsible for communicating concerns about a student's intellectual habits directly to the student?

4. Are a student's "style" and an instructor's "style" ever so discordant that a certain student simply should not be in class with a certain instructor?

5. "Some students have a lot of baggage..." the instructor muses at the end of this case, "there's not much I can do to help them." Can an instructor realistically be expected to explore and respond to all of his or her students' "baggage"?

6. Is the instructor's conclusion about "baggage" at the end of the case an accurate assessment of the events?

To Hell in a Handbasket:
The Case of the Failed Group Project
Regina Lopata Logan

Somewhere on the north side of a large midwestern city, in a yellow-brick bungalow, Emma Black sank into her chair with a loud sigh. "Why the heck did they wait til now to call?" she murmured to herself.

"Whadya say, Mom?" her teenaged son asked.

"Oh, nothing, honey. Well, actually, it's one of my students. He just now, one week before the end of the semester, decided to tell me how much trouble his group is having on their project. And, he says, he thinks the other groups are floundering, too."

Meanwhile, in the western suburbs of that same city, George O'Riley slammed the door of his mini-van and stormed into the house. "Anybody here?" he yelled, half-hoping no one would respond so that he could have a minute to collect his thoughts. Unfortunately for George, however, two pug dogs, an alley cat, and a sleepy toddler all came tumbling to his feet as his wife called from the kitchen, "You're late! I'm out here!" As soon as she saw his face, she knew he was upset. "What's wrong?" she inquired, as he gave her a quick peck on the cheek.

"That stupid final project! It's really a joke. I stayed at the office to call Ms. Black — Emma — to tell her our group is going to hell in a handbasket... ."

The next day, Emma tried to figure out what had happened; how had she seemingly blown the major assignmentshe had given her class. Emma taught marketing in the evening school of a large, prestigious university. She, herself, had twenty years of marketing experience: fifteen with a large corporation in the food industry, and five with a consulting firm that specialized in merchandising and marketing new products. She had been teaching for six years, usually one course per semester. Teaching kept her sharp and was a great way for her to share her expertise. And, according to her student evaluations, she was a pretty good teacher. Her students were anywhere from their early twenties to mid-fifties; many had degrees and experience in the field of marketing. Each time she taught the advanced course in marketing, she thought, this year, I'm going to give them a group project as the culmination of the semester's work. She had never actually assigned a project, although she did like to break into small groups for discussion and problem-solving exercises. This year, she decided the course would culminate in a group project/paper. After careful consideration, she wrote the following assignment, given out at the seventh week of a fourteen-week semester:

> For the next seven weeks, you will work on a group project that will encompass a presentation and paper. I will divide the class into groups of five; each group will choose its own marketing dilemma and write up a proposal to solve the problem, basing the paper on both research and experience. You will have part of each class to work on your project. The last night of class, each group will make a fifteen-minute presentation, using whatever visual aids you wish. Your final paper will be a summary of your research. It should be at least twenty pages long, typed, double-spaced. You will need to have at least ten references as part of your research.

Emma was pleased with her assignment. She felt it was a good opportunity for her students to experience a project that they were likely to encounter in real-life marketing jobs.

The night she handed out the assignment, several students groaned, but she figured "you can't please all of the people all of the time." One of her better students, a manufacturer's rep, who was hoping to move into marketing after he finished his degree, was the first to raise his hand.

"Yes, George, what is your question?"

"Would you explain how you're going to grade us?"

Oh, for Pete's sake, Emma thought to herself, the old grading thing. You'd think adults wouldn't be so worried about grades! After all, it's the learning that counts! For what seemed like the thousandth time in her career, she began, "Well, George, I think you all know that grading isn't as important as the actual process. When you work in a group, there's a lot of learning that goes on. It creates a real life experience: learning how to delegate the workload and being responsible for your share. It will be clear to all of you how you're doing and it will certainly be clear to me when you make your presentation. Don't worry about it now; I'm sure it will all come together by the end of the semester."

George lowered his head so she wouldn't see his expression. He was truly annoyed, but no one else was saying anything, so he just kept quiet.

Later, at the break, several students came up to him to say they hated group projects and they never worked, anyway, but no one brought anything up when class reconvened.

At the tenth week, Emma thought the projects seemed to be going well. Each group had handed in the description of a marketing problem they were going to tackle. They also handed in a weekly assessment sheet she had devised: a checklist outlining what they were currently working on. She had given them thirty minutes at the end of class last week and would give them some time again tonight and next week. And she was sure they could communicate with each other by e-mail and fax during the week.

George was getting really ticked off by his group. First, there was Alice, a very laid-back design major who didn't seem to care too much about marketing, and had declared that she wasn't used to working with others so they would just have to remind her what she was supposed to do. Bill and Glenn, two other members of the group, were pretty motivated. However, Bill travelled more in his job than George did, and George travelled two or three days a week. Bill wanted to do his share, but it just seemed like he was always on the road. Glenn worked part time as a service representative for an insurance company and the rest of the time, he cared for his two preschoolers while his wife worked as a nurse, sometimes in the day and sometimes at night. Glenn's schedule was really unpredictable. To complicate matters, he wasn't on-line at home, and when he was at his job, he felt uncomfortable as a part-timer using his e-mail and fax for non-company business. Marilyn, the other member of their group, was at the other end of the spectrum. She was a vice-president at a medium-sized paper company, and was shifting from personnel to marketing. She was so intense and so keyed up that just being around her made George anxious. She not only did her part, she was interested in doing Alice's and everyone else's, too. George felt discouraged and overwhelmed by his group's inability to work together. They never had enough time in class. Last week, Emma had given them the last thirty-five minutes of class, but she left after the first ten minutes, asking whoever was the last to leave, to be sure to turn off the classroom lights. About two minutes after she left, several students started to pack up their things and within five more minutes, no one was left in the room, except George and Marilyn. Marilyn assured George that she had almost completed the PowerPoint presentation; she just was waiting for Glenn to get the last bits of data to her. They only needed a few minutes, she was sure. But George's group wasn't able to meet any time outside of class. Alice and Bill lived in the city, but one lived north and one lived south. As for the others, no one even lived in the same suburb as anyone else!

By the end of the thirteenth week, with the project and paper due the following week, George had just about given up. He decided he better call Emma and tell her what a fiasco this whole thing was turning out to be!

Questions:
1. What, if anything, did Emma do correctly to set up the group project?
2. How can a group project be graded equitably?
3. What can students do to inform the teacher about the progress in a group project?

Bridging a Gap
Sandra Basile

Linda is from Australia, but has been living in the United States for two years with Tom, her American husband. At first she thought the move to the States would not require significant adjustment. After all, she grew up with American movies, news, television shows, and music. In addition, Linda made several trips to the United States to visit Tom's family before they were married. She thought she knew all she needed to know about America.

Linda works as a personnel assistant for a large manufacturing company. Although she finds the work rewarding, she has experienced some subtle cultural shocks. For example, during her first few weeks, Linda learned that Americans address their top management formally, using a surname. In Australia, regardless of a person's social or professional status, everyone uses first names. Even the Prime Minister of Australia could be addressed by his first name in many situations.

Linda, who took several university courses in Australia, decided to return to school to enhance her professional knowledge and perhaps pursue a Bachelor's degree. A logical place to begin, she thought, was an HRD class. Because of her experience, she decided to pass up the beginning human resource management class in favor of a class in training and development.

* * * * *

The instructor's name was Ken Benton. On the first night of class, Ken presented the course outline, went over the reading material, and explained how the students would be graded. Next, he gave a brief description of the exams. Linda followed the explanation with interest.

After describing the course, Ken explained that this was the first class he had taught. However, he said, he had extensive professional experience and proceeded to list his academic credentials, explain his fifteen years of work experience, and note some of his awards.

Linda was surprised at the pride Ken appeared to show in his achievements. She had never seen an Australian teacher show such pride. To do so would run the risk of being considered a "tall poppy"— someone who needed to be cut down to the same level as others. In Australia, teachers and other professionals do not give their credentials like a resume. Instead, a person's qualifications are shown through his or her actions.

After introducing himself, Ken asked how many people were taking an evening class at the university for the first time. More than half of the students raised their hands. Although Ken seemed surprised at this response, he said they would learn the "night school ropes" together. He asked the students to go around the room, stating their names, where they worked, and why they were taking the class. When Linda spoke, Ken asked her where she was from. When she told him, he welcomed her to her first American college course. Linda felt a little better that he understood she was from another country.

After the introductions, Ken explained what he thought the students could expect to learn and what he would be expecting from them. To give the students an example of his expectations, and to wind up the class for that evening, he said, he wanted the class to do a simple case study.

He split the class into three groups and told the students that each group represented an HRD consultant hired by a company to help select which departments in a medium-sized corporation should be trained first in new telecommunications technologies. He handed out a one-page case, which described the company and the various departments from which employees might be chosen.

All he wanted, Ken said, was for the groups to think of ways the company could implement a training program— for example, suggest what departments should be targeted first and what means they would use to train the employees from those areas. He said he would give the groups five minutes to study the case and come up with their ideas. Then one person from each group would stand in front of the class to discuss the group's solution.

Linda found herself in a group that had never done a case study before. No one was sure what to do. They read the case; after that, most of the group members just sat quietly. Linda flagged down Ken and asked what they should do. He said, "It's a very simple case. Just give ideas from your own experience on how you would select certain departments and train the chosen employees. And remember no answer is right or wrong."

Linda decided to take the initiative. She told the others what department she would choose as a pilot and what kind of training she would use.

Mike, another member of Linda's group, suggested another department.

Linda shook her head. "No. Why would you want to include that department?"

Mike seemed a bit stunned. "I thought everyone had the right to at least express an idea and have the group consider it."

When Ken told the groups to wrap up their discussions, Mike told Linda, "I think you should be the spokesperson. You seem to understand the case better than anyone else in the group."

"Okay," Ken said. "Group One. What did you come up with?"

Linda finished writing her notes and hurried to the front of the room. At first, she felt uncomfortable with all these Americans looking at her. She was afraid she would start using Australian expressions and embarrass herself or confuse the students.

She summarized the case and then presented her ideas about solving the company's training problem. She felt less nervous as she spoke and, when she finished, she started back to her seat with a sense of satisfaction.

Ken stopped her. "You're not finished yet. Stay there. I want to ask you some questions."

Her nervousness returned and Linda returned to the front of the room. Ken asked several questions about the group's solutions. However, as Linda tried to answer each question, Ken would start to tap his foot, say, "Okay, okay," and ask another question.

Finally Ken said the group had done well on the first part of the case, but less well on the second part. Linda glanced toward the other students and saw that Mike was smiling and looking satisfied.

Linda turned back to Ken. "You only gave us five minutes to examine the case. It's too much to expect us to give you so much detail after studying the case for such a short time."

Ken did not reply directly. With Linda still standing at the front of the room, he turned to the class and presented his ideas about solving the case.

When he finished, Linda said, "I can't believe you would recommend that approach for this company to follow."

Ken raised both eyebrows. When he replied, his tone was firm. "Linda, I have fifteen years of HRD experience. In the real world, this is a common approach. In fact, this case was drawn from one of my early experiences."

"Well," Linda said, "I'm sure you had more than five minutes to develop your solution. But my group's solution is a good one. It covers the major points rather than concentrating on the minute details."

Ken's jaw was clamped and his cheeks were showing red. "Linda, I think you are missing the major point of this case. I'm trying to explain that point to you. This is an easy case, but for the past ten minutes you have made it more difficult than it was intended to be. I want to move on now, so please sit down."

As Linda sat, she found herself confused about Ken's

reaction. In her Australian classes, instructors always had been comfortable having ideas challenged. It was nothing personal, as Ken's reaction seemed to suggest; it was simply a discussion of ideas. If Ken wanted to avoid such a debate, perhaps he wasn't qualified to teach the class, Linda thought.

Linda glanced around the room. The other students appeared uncomfortable.

"We need to get the other groups up here," Ken said. "They can present their ideas, but we won't have time to discuss them. Maybe we can continue the discussion next time."

Representatives of the next two groups spoke about their findings, and, as promised, Ken did not question them.

As Linda headed for the door at the end of class, she noticed that Ken was looking rather grim. For her part, she planned to check the university catalog when she got home to see whether she could still drop the class and what others she might take instead. Perhaps, she thought, the introductory HRD class would be a better choice. Or perhaps another discipline altogether.

Questions:

1. To what extent are cultural differences responsible for the difficulties encountered during this first class meeting?
2. To what extent is the instructor responsible for recognizing and adapting to these differences? How could he do so?
3. To what extent is the student responsible for bridging this cultural gap? How might she do so?
4. What other factors contributed to the difficulties in this situation?
5. What steps could the student take, if she decides to return to class?
6 What steps could the instructor take now to improve the situation?
7. In what ways might the difficulties shown here occur even when a student—particularly an adult student—is a lifelong resident of the United States?

Real Work

Cecilia M. Germaine

Michael Bradington, as he usually did, began the class in management techniques with an overview of what he planned to accomplish during the current semester, explaining what would be expected of the students in terms of reading, special projects, and class participation. He particularly emphasized the latter. "Approximately 30 percent of your grade in this class will be based on your participation in class discussions," he told the assembled students. "I expect everyone to be an active participant." Dr. Bradington was particularly well qualified to teach this class. In fact, he had been responsible for the development of the management techniques curriculum for the college, the evening division of a large university. He had held senior management positions in several national and international corporations, and for the last fifteen years had worked as a private management consultant. He had been teaching this particular course for ten years.

"I really hope I do well in this class, but I'm afraid I'm not off to a very good start," said Rita Simmons to a small group of her fellow students as they chatted during the class break. It was the first night of the fall semester, and Rita was nervous. After a long absence, she was returning to school to complete her degree and she was concerned about this big step. Her classmates offered words of encouragement, recounting their own stories about going back to school, their first classes, and adjusting to college life as an adult.

Rita was grateful for the support of her classmates, but she was still filled with doubts about her ability to hold her own in this new environment. In her mind she played back the scene that had occurred at the beginning of the class.

All of the students had been asked by Michael Bradington to introduce themselves and tell the class something about what they did when they weren't in night school. Rita listened in dismay as her classmates gave their names and told about their jobs. Every person in the class, with the exception of herself, was employed in a responsible position, and many worked for large corporations. Dr. Bradington seemed fascinated by the variety and extent of the students' careers. He asked most of them several questions about the kinds of functions they performed and what management experience they had. He jotted down a few notes after each student with a slight smile or nod of his head, implying how impressed he was at their expertise. Finally it was Rita's turn to stand.

"My name is Rita Simmons," she began. "For the past six years I have been at home with my two children."

"So you don't work?" queried Michael Bradington. "That's very interesting. I hope you'll be able to keep up with the class." He then raised his eyebrows at the person to Rita's left, indicating he should proceed with his introduction. Rita felt her face flush dark red with embarrassment. Dr. Bradington had cut her off before she could relate her job experience prior to the birth of her first child.

After class Rita and Julie Altman walked together to the parking lot. "I'm more nervous than ever about this class," Rita confided to Julie. "I know I've been out of the work force for a while, but before the kids, I had lots of great experience! I worked in the human resource department of a large accounting firm. At first, I was an employment counselor, and later I was promoted to mediator in staff-management problems. And since I've been at home, I've helped my husband run his restaurant. It's true that my primary focus has been on my children, but it took a lot of sacrifice to live on one salary—and I'm not about to feel guilty about being a mother! Now that the baby is in first grade, I'm ready to go back to work. I thought that if I got a master's degree it would be a plus. I took this class because it sounded interesting, and I thought it would be a good way to ease my way back into school before I take the GMATs."

"You'll do fine, Rita," Julie responded. "Just because you haven't been holding down a paying job doesn't mean that you've lost your ability to. Besides, raising kids requires plenty of management techniques! And it isn't as though you've never worked before." Rita thanked Julie for her encouragement, but as she headed home she was still upset. All she could think about was that she just couldn't compete with all those other students — and how much Dr. Bradington had humiliated her.

Rita went to the second session ready to become an active member of the class. The subject of the lecture and discussion was problem employees. She had read the assigned cases and thought about a similar situation she had encountered at the accounting firm. "I know I'll be able to offer some good ideas during our discussion tonight," she thought as she drove to campus.

In class Michael Bradington spoke for about 30 minutes and then began to lead the class into a discussion of the case he had presented. "I know that not all of you are in the work force and may not be able to relate to this problem," he said, glancing at Rita. "Just do the best you can," he added in a resigned voice.

Rita blushed and slumped in her seat. She remained silent during the discussion period.

"I don't know what to do," Rita said to Julie as they walked to their cars after class. "Dr. Bradington clearly doesn't think I have anything to contribute to this class."

"Why don't you make an appointment with him?" responded Julie. "Just explain to him how his remarks make you feel and ask him to stop."

"I couldn't do that, Julie. He would probably resent it and I would ruin any chance I have for a good grade in his class." Rita fumbled with her car keys, blinking back tears of anger and disappointment. "Maybe going back to school was just a stupid idea, anyway... ." Her voice trailed off.

"Well, I think you should do something. If you're uncomfortable talking to Dr. Bradington, why not talk to one of the deans in the college? Sue Richards is a good person, easy to talk to, and I think you'll find her sympathetic to your situation." Julie smiled reassuringly.

"Thanks, Julie. I'll think about it." They waved at each other as they pulled out of their parking spaces. Yes, I will think about it—a lot! Rita vowed to herself.

A few days later Rita called Sue Richards and set up an appointment to discuss her problem. "Dr. Richards," Rita began, "I'm about ready to drop this management techniques class. I don't want to look like a quitter, but I'm afraid Dr. Bradington doesn't take me as seriously as he does the other students."

"Tell me exactly what's happening," Sue Richards responded.

"I've been nervous about going back to school, but since I have some experience in this field, I thought the management class would be a good way to build my confidence. The problem is, Dr. Bradington seems to think that my not holding down a 'real' job recently is a detriment to my ability to do well. I feel he is singling me out by repeatedly referring to my unemployment. As result, I'm reluctant to participate in the class discussions, and I know that will have a serious effect on my grade. I need to do well in this class, and I just don't see how I can, given Dr. Bradington's attitude toward me." It all came out in sort of a rush, but Rita felt relieved to have everything out in the open.

"Rita, don't give up so quickly. Let me have a talk with Dr. Bradington. He is an excellent teacher, and he may not realize how you are interpreting his comments." Dean Richards again assured Rita that this was atypical behavior for Dr. Bradington and they parted with Sue's promise to get back to Rita within several days.

Later that week Sue Richards met with Michael Bradington. "Michael," Sue began, "Rita Simmons came to see me the other day. She is feeling very unsure about being in your class, and thinks that because of her lack of recent work experience you're not taking her as seriously as you do the other students."

Michael leaned back in his chair and put his fingertips together. "Sue, the work place today is far different from the time Rita was actively employed. Business techniques have changed. Businesses expect more of everyone, and a long time out of the work force can be a huge disadvantage. There are too many women who have been steadily employed with whom she will be competing for a job. I'm trying to do her a favor."

"I'm sure you mean well, Michael, but isn't there some other technique you can use to get your point across?"

Questions:
1. How else might Michael help Rita understand the current workplace?
2. What can Rita do to establish her credibility in this class?
3. How can returning homemakers transfer their practical knowledge to the classroom?
4. What can instructors do to "level the playing field" between highly experienced and less experienced students?

Part IV:
Cases from an Administrative
Perspective

Freedom: Principles and Paradoxes
Louise Love

When Peter Bolonsky retired from the political science department of Independence State University, he resolved to keep his hand in teaching by offering courses through the adult program in the evening. He had always had an interest in adult students and in ISU's University College, but his work with doctoral students and his ambitious program of research and publication kept him from taking on any additional teaching. Now that he was officially "retired" he felt he could test some of his theories of adult education and realize a goal that he had set aside for many years. The continuing education division was delighted to receive this distinguished scholar and emeritus professor into the University College teaching corps. University College Dean Carole Sherman asked Bolonsky to teach the capstone seminar for political science majors — a research course for which the topic varied from year to year. For his first seminar, Bolonsky chose the topic "Freedom of Speech: Principles and Paradoxes." Enrollment for the class was limited to fifteen, and the course closed early in the registration period.

A practice of ISU's University College was to administer midterm evaluations for "new" faculty after the first seven weeks of class. Dean Sherman was concerned, when she hired Bolonsky, that he might be offended by being treated as a "new" faculty member when he had had a teaching career with the College of Liberal Arts and Sciences for almost three decades, and she contemplated waiving this procedure in Bolonsky's case. As it happened, however, the dean did not have to wait until midterm to get her first reaction to Bolonsky's course.

After the first week of classes, the Registrar's Office reported an unusual number of drops from the Bolonsky seminar (four out of fifteen students), and the Academic Review Board received a petition requesting a full refund from a disappointed student. In the petition, the student said that the teacher hadn't taught them anything and wasn't planning to. There was no syllabus, the student claimed, no assignments, and no method of grading. In addition, the student wrote, "The teacher didn't say anything on the first meeting of the class. He just sat there. I paid $850 for this course because I expected to be taught something. Obviously, this is not going to happen, and I want my money back." Sherman reluctantly placed a call to Bolonsky. She felt uneasy questioning the teaching of this distinguished emeritus professor—but she had to check out this very unlikely account of his first class.

Bolonsky's explanation of what took place on the first night of class reassured Dean Sherman to some extent, but she determined that it would be a good idea to administer the midterm evaluations in any case. Bolonsky explained that he had not said anything at the beginning of class because he wanted to engage the students immediately in the principles and paradoxes of freedom of speech. He wanted to illustrate the power of an authoritarian system to silence speech even when there was no explicit inhibitor. He wanted to see (and have the students see) how much time would elapse before someone took responsibility for breaking the silence and offering something—anything—an explanation of what was happening, a reaction to what was happening, an idea, some information, a theory—anything. Bolonsky was practicing both active learning and a simulation exercise as a way of engaging the students in free speech issues. He told Sherman that he had successfully used this and other experiments with his graduate students and had long wanted to try his techniques with adult undergraduates.

Bolonsky explained that, although he had not said anything for the first half of the class, he had written in large letters on the board, "Who am I? What do I want?" to stimulate the students to think about their goals for the class and to think about the exercise in which they were engaged.

Realizing that in a University College class he might be

mistaken for one of the students, Bolonsky sat at the teacher's desk so that his presence would be unambiguous. Bolonsky told Sherman that the class had sat in silence with only side conversation among individual students for a little over a half hour. After that time, a male student — probably in his late twenties or early thirties — spoke up and said, "Well, I guess I'll start. I'm a graduating senior with a major in political science. This course is the last requirement for my major. I was really happy when I saw that the topic this year was freedom of speech because I want to learn more about the First Amendment and, specifically, about the extent to which Marxists deny its reality. I have read some of the professor's articles and I think it's great that I'll be taking my last course with him." No one else spoke, and then the same student added, "I'm also applying to graduate programs in political science, and I wouldn't mind getting a letter of recommendation from Professor Bolonsky. I'm sure it would help a lot." The student blushed and laughed and was quiet.

Several other students then spoke up and said who they were and what they hoped to get from the class. One said he was not a degree candidate at all. He already had a graduate degree in business. He said that he had decided to take a course at University College so he wouldn't go "brain dead." He chose Professor Bolonsky's course because the subject just sounded interesting. Another student said that she was a journalism major and was interested in issues of censorship. Another said that he was a business major and needed a social science course. And he added, "One that meets on Wednesday nights." Another said that she was interested in policies concerning "hate speech" on college campuses.

Bolonsky told Sherman that, after the break, several students did not return. "And that's all right," Bolonsky said, "That's as it should be. Students should be allowed to shop around for the classes they want to take." Dean Sherman thought (but did not say) that these students weren't just "shopping." They were actually registered and had already paid tuition. The "budget" side of her mind considered the fact that, in order to make the budget, the average class size had to be fifteen. Any course with a lower enrollment was not entirely "pulling its weight." This was not, of course, the dean's primary concern at the moment because plenty of classes had over fifteen students. The school could afford to carry classes with enrollments lower than fifteen without putting the "bottom line" in any real jeopardy. But she was not pleased with Bolonsky's cavalier attitude toward drops.

In their conversation about the first class meeting, Bolonsky told Sherman that he had a great deal of respect for adult learners and did not want to dictate the content of the course to them. Not did he want to stifle their intellectual agendas by asserting himself as the "expert." He wanted to conduct class like a graduate seminar in which students could identify research areas of their own particular interest; conduct a study; report findings to the group; elicit help from the teacher and the other students on solving problems that emerged while doing the study; and, ultimately, write a paper discussing the problem, the process, and whatever findings or conclusions had emerged from the study. He said he believed, like William James, that teachers should instill in students a "devouring curiosity" and allow the students' intellectual energy to drive the curriculum. For that reason, he had not created a syllabus for the class. "That would have been arrogance on my part," he explained. "My job is to create a space in which students can experience themselves as inquiring beings and learn to take responsibility for that drive and to satisfy it."

Bolonsky explained that, after the break on the first night of class, he had distributed a thirty-page annotated bibliography that was organized around various research topics. For the following week, the students were asked to read the bibliography, browse in the library—both electronically and in the stacks—and bring to class preliminary ideas for their research projects. In addition, students were asked to find at least one article from a newspaper or journal that related issues of free speech to current events—either in the United States or abroad. He asked the students to make copies of the article for each member of the class and come prepared to lead a brief discussion of the article and the issues that it raised.

Dean Sherman was relieved to learn that Bolonsky had done considerably more than simply "sit there"—as the petitioner for a full refund suggested. Clearly, Bolonsky had a plan in mind and some educational theory to back it up. She checked the Change of Registration forms of the three other students who had abandoned the class. Under "Reason for Drop/Add" one student wrote "change in work schedule"; another wrote "chose another class"; and the third wrote nothing at all. Sherman knew that students did not always report their real reasons for dropping a class, and felt that she could draw no conclusion about the students' reaction to Bolonsky's "experiment" from the information given on these forms. She advised the Academic Review Board to give the petitioning student his money back; although, deep down she did not believe that this was really justified. Above all, she hoped that, by authorizing one refund, she would not start a stampede of other "drops" seeking to get their money back as well.

* * * * *

The first thing that Carole Sherman did on the Thursday morning after midterm evaluations had been administered in the Wednesday night classes, was to look at what had been written by Professor Bolonsky's students (now down to ten). For the most part, the evaluations were far better than what the dean had feared. Several students praised the format of the class that allowed them to pursue their own interests and set their own learning goals. One commented, "Prof. Bolonsky is brilliant. It is an honor to study with him." Another wrote, "The professor respects the students. I appreciate his high standards and expectations." Although most of the students seemed to be thriving in Bolonsky's class, several of the evaluations expressed less-than-enthusiastic reactions. One student wrote, "The class is not well organized. The teacher has no plan. I need this course to graduate, and I am concerned about my grade." Another wrote, "I didn't need to spend money to listen to other students talk. If I wanted to teach myself, I could have done that for free. It's too late to drop now, but I wish I had switched to another class earlier." Sherman looked up the Change of Registration form for the fifth student who dropped the class. Under "Reason for Drop/Add" it simply said "personal." Sherman wondered what that really meant.

Concerned about the students who were having difficulty with Bolonsky's teaching method, Sherman decided to call her friend, Wendy Denham, an assistant professor in the political science department, and ask what she knew about Bolonsky. Denham was famous both for her cutting "put-downs" and also for her consuming ambition. Nevertheless, her response took Sherman by surprise. "Bolonsky? Ohmigod. He was the laziest man in the department. He never lifted a finger for his classes— put the whole thing off on the students and couched it in pedagogical mumbo-jumbo. The gossip in the department was that he did everything he could do to get students to drop his classes so he could just work with a few at a time. The department could never get him to do any committee work, an, when he was chair of the department, the department assistant did everything. She couldn't even reach him by phone most of the time."

"But," Sherman asked, "What about his reputation as a scholar?"

"Well, yes," conceded Denham, "Whatever energy he had, he spent on his writing — but a lot of the credit for his work belongs to his graduate students. The graduate students flocked to him in spite of everything because he took good care of the ones he favored. He introduced them around at conferences, helped them get articles published, and, yes, he really did help them get jobs. He has cronies all over the country, and a recommendation from him can mean a lot to a new Ph.D. on the job market."

Sherman made an appointment to speak in person with Bolonsky. He asked her to meet him in his office. When she arrived, Bolonsky started in talking before Sherman had even had a chance to sit down. "I am enjoying teaching for University College immensely—as I knew I would. These adult students are as bright as any so-called "regular students" that I've ever had—and so motivated! They are tireless. I am looking forward to reading their final papers. I think it's even possible that some of them might be suitable for publication."

During the ensuing conversation, Dean Sherman tried to suggest to Bolonsky that some of the students seemed to be struggling and might benefit from a little more structure. She pointed out that not all of the students in the class were political science majors with intellectual agendas of their own; indeed, some of them were taking the course for elective credit. One student, she reminded him, was taking it purely for enrichment. That student might have appreciated a set of assigned readings, she ventured.

Bolonsky listened to Sherman, but ended by reassuring her that he knew exactly what he was doing. "You'll see," he said. "My students don't always understand my methods at the time—and that goes for my graduate students as well—but, in time, they come to appreciate that there's 'method in my madness.' " Sherman looked at the floor and could feel herself blushing. Had Bolonsky heard that she was checking up on him?

He laughed jovially, stood up, and dismissed Sherman. As she was leaving, he called after her, "Remember the words of Goddard: 'A teacher who infuriates a student is better than a machine that leaves him stuffed with information but cold as a mackerel.' I don't think you'll find any mackerels in my class." Sherman thought, "If there is anyone left in your class."

Back in her office, Sherman thought about a keynote address that she had heard at a national conference a few years earlier. The speaker was Stephen Brookfield, a teacher of teachers whose ideas Sherman had come to admire. In his keynote address, Brookfield had described his own development as a teacher in which he had learned to exercise his authority and his expertise contrary to his own inclination, which had been to give the students control of the class. Sherman took one of Brookfield's books from her shelf and tried to find a passage that might be of help. When she found it, she made a copy and sent it to Bolonsky — again, hoping she was not going too far. The passage read as follows:

> The conversations with my students about their experiences in my classes surprised and alarmed me. I discovered that my tendency to downplay my own knowledge and experience in an effort to reduce the distance between us only served to widen it. My dismissal of what I knew and could do was not always perceived as reassuringly self-deprecating. Sometimes, it created an unnecessary degree of anxiety in already insecure students. I was implying that there was no real point in their showing up to my class, since they were not going to learn anything from me anyway. I was also unwittingly insulting the seriousness of their educational intentions.
>
> I found out, too, that my tendency to let discussion flow with minimal interruption on my part (a reflection of my respect for students' voices and my desire to encourage their articulation of their own experiences in their own terms) was sometimes interpreted by students as my way of avoiding any declaration of my own agenda or concerns. Students told me that my unwillingness to intervene too directly in class discussions for fear of overemphasizing the power of my own voice was actually allowing for the perpetuation of differences of class, race, and gender that existed outside of the classroom. My occasional refusal to give clear directions for assignments and exercises sometimes appeared duplicitous and manipulative, rather than the respectful prompt of self-directedness I had intended.

Two days after sending this passage to Bolonsky, Sherman received a letter back in the intercampus mail. With some trepidation, she opened the envelope and found a photocopied page with the following passage highlighted. The page was identified as having been copied from Bill Reading's *The University in Ruins*.

> Educated properly, the subject learns the rules of thought, not a content of positive knowledge, so that thought and knowledge acquisition become a freely autonomous activity, part of the subject... . The teacher does not transmit facts...but rather does two things. First, the teacher narrativizes the search for knowledge, tells the story of the process of knowledge acquisition. Second, the teacher enacts the process, sets knowledge to work. What is taught thus is not just facts but critique—the formal art of the use of mental powers, the process of judgment.

Across the top of the page, Bolonsky had written only the following, "Who is Stephen Brookfield?"

* * * * *

At the end of the semester, Bolonsky sent Sherman two of the papers from the class with a Post-It note saying "Voila! —P.B." Sherman had to agree that they were exceptionally good papers: the theses were clearly articulated, the research was impressive and well documented, and the arguments were coherent and persuasive. "Yes," she said to herself. "He really did get good work from the students."

Sherman read the evaluations that had been written by the students on the penultimate class meeting. There were now nine students in the class, and six of the nine gave the class high ratings — with comments like "Challenging," "I've never worked so hard and I loved it," "I'm sorry that the course is over. This was the best class I've taken in five years as a University College student." Two of the evaluations were mixed; and one complained bitterly about the class, especially about the vagueness of grading standards.

After the grades were sent to students, Sherman received a grade appeal from one of Bolonsky's nine remaining students. With the letter was a copy of the student's final paper and several short written assignments that had been done in class. There was also a final exam with only one essay question which read, "Create your own essay question and answer it. Ask yourself a question that allows you to reflect on a paradox or principle relating to freedom of speech other than that on which you wrote your paper." None of the papers had a grade or any other notations from the teacher on them.

In the letter of appeal, the student wrote, "The grade I received was unfair because there were no clearly articulated standards for grading. We never received a syllabus, and the teacher never explained how our grades would be determined. All he ever said was that he would base our grades on the quality of our project and how well we succeeded in meeting our own intellectual goals. He never even told us that there would be a final exam. I did everything that the teacher asked, came to every class except two (even though going was a total waste of my time) and I worked hard on my final paper. I didn't do as well as I could have on my final exam because I was so upset when he told us we were having one. I know that the teacher didn't like me because I challenged his teaching style and called him at home because he didn't keep any office hours. I just wanted to get more information from him and find out how I was doing in the class. Once, when I asked him specifically how I was doing in the class, he told me to stop worrying about it. He said the grade was not important. But it is important to me because I don't want my GPA to be brought down by one lousy professor. He gave me a B- because he had a grudge against me. For all the work I did in the class, I believe I deserve an A. Especially since I basically taught myself anyway. If anyone deserves to give out grades for the course it's the other students because they did all the teaching."

Sherman sighed knowing that she would be having another conversation with Bolonsky to discuss the grading standards used in the class. She also needed to respond to his proposal to teach another seminar in the coming year. The topic he had proposed for the next year's capstone seminar was, "Political Theory and Educational Philosophy." Dean Sherman pondered what she should do. What, she wondered, would Stephen Brookfield advise her to do?

References:

Brookfield, S. D. (1995). *Becoming a critically reflective teacher* (xi-xii). San Francisco: Jossey-Bass.

Readings, B. (1996). *The university in ruins* (p. 67). Harvard University Press. Quoted in Stanley Katz, "Can Liberal Education Cope?" an address to the Association of Graduate Liberal Studies Programs, October 30, 1997.

Questions:

1. Should Dean Sherman have been more assertive in her interactions with professor Bolonsky? What might she have done to assess his teaching methods before the end of the semester?
2. Discuss the two educational philosophies mentioned in this case: Brookfield's and Reading's. What are the strenghts and weaknesses of each philosophy?
3. If you were Dean Sherman, would you hire Bolonsky to teach again? If so, would you make any directives about how he should teach? If not, how would you justify your decision in light of academic freedom?

The Case of the Mixed Message
Hilary Ward Schnadt

It was the fourth week of the fall semester. When the phone rang, Assistant Dean Margaret Smith didn't even wince. Most of the registration problems had been solved, the semester was up and running, she could even see actual desk surface beneath the sheaves of papers that needed dealing with.

"This is Jane Ostrowski. I'm a student in Psychology C14, special topics, taught by Jennifer Noonan, and I would like to come in and speak with you about some problems with the course and the teacher."

Student/teacher problems were nothing new to Dean Smith. Mostly they involved clashing expectations and students fearful of raising the problem with the teacher. She recognized the teacher's name and knew her to be a doctoral student teaching for University College for the first time. Dean Smith tried to draw the student out over the phone, but Jane was insistent that they talk in person. She set an appointment with the student for the following day.

Jane arrived promptly the next day for her appointment. Dean Smith waved her into one of the armchairs in her office and took a seat in the other. She prepared to do a little coaching on raising issues of unmet expectations with teachers in a non-confrontational way. Although close to half of the University College students had degrees already, many were back in college working on undergraduate degrees after a lengthy absence from academe. Often they were unsure of their own abilities and awkward about student/teacher dynamics.

But Jane launched into the discussion promptly. "Thank you for meeting with me, Dean Smith. I want you to know that I don't usually complain about teachers and the way they conduct class. I have a B.S. in microbiology and chemistry, and a number of graduate credits already. I'm taking this upper-level psychology course as part of my preparation to apply for medical school.

"Given my educational background, I think I'm well-versed in reading scientific literature. However, the 'text' of this course is a packet of scientific articles that are extremely difficult to understand. The problem is that Jennifer Noonan just doesn't teach. The first week, she took attendance, outlined the course and showed a movie. We all looked at each other, but we figured, 'How much can you do on the first night?' For the second week, we had two difficult articles to read. I read and reread them, but I still didn't feel confident that I understood them.

"When I got to class, I expected it to be like all the other classes I'd had which involved highly technical, scientific literature. I expected the teacher to teach it! I thought she'd lecture on the articles, or at least outline their concepts for us. Instead, she said something like, 'In case you did not follow the most significant points, I will read them to you.' That was very condescending! I haven't been read to since I was in grade school." She stopped, suddenly realizing how much louder her voice had gotten as she recounted her frustration.

"Did you express your frustration to the teacher?" Dean Smith asked.

"Yes, I did. And so did the rest of the class. We had a very heated discussion about the format of the class. We told her that we weren't understanding the articles and that we wanted her to lecture more and to give us more context for understanding them. I probably have about the most background in this field. Some of the other students were asking for definitions of some of the terms in the articles and outlines of the articles themselves."

"What was Jennifer's response?"

"She said that she did not set this course up to be a lecture course. She expected us to be able to read the articles and discuss them. I had to miss the third week of class, but I'm told that she broke the class into small groups to synopsize and discuss the articles. How can we discuss them when we don't understand them?"

Dean Smith allowed as how that might pose a problem.

"Last night, for the fourth class session, she wasn't even there. She sent a substitute instead. Dean Smith, Jennifer Noonan just isn't teaching this course and she gets very defensive about it when we try to discuss it with her. Since 25% of our final grade is based on class participation, a lot of us are very nervous. One, how can we participate when we can't understand the material? Two, if we keep talking to her about the course, we're afraid she's going to hold it against us in our grades. I need a high grade for my medical school application. I want these problems on record now, in case I have to make a grade appeal later.

"Also, there's another student in the class who's talking about filing a petition to have the teacher replaced. What's the chance that we can get a new teacher?"

Dean Smith sat silent for a moment. She'd never had a student ask about replacing the teacher mid-semester. Clearly, that was not going to happen, but a student-circulated petition requesting it might do more to damage the classroom dynamics than oral complaints.

"Well, Jane, I'm afraid that there's no possibility that we would replace the teacher in the middle of the semester. Our teachers have a contract with us, which we have to honor. However, we have a very strong faculty development program, because we have so many graduate student instructors who are new to teaching. I'll speak with the coordinator of the program and we'll see if we can intervene to get the course on track. There are still ten more weeks of the term. I'm glad you came in to express your concerns now, while we still have time to try to fix things. I wouldn't encourage your fellow student to circulate a petition, but here are some of my cards. If other students have concerns, they can feel free to call me with them."

Jane seemed only slightly mollified and took with her a complaint form to put her objections on paper. After walking the student to the elevator, Dean Smith retrieved her afternoon's mail from her mailbox. One letter was marked "personal and confidential." Opening it first, Dean Smith discovered that it was from a student in the same class.

The letter introduced the writer as Jim Goodman, a student in his third course toward matriculating into a degree program. His academic adviser encouraged him to write to Dean Smith about the problems in this course. He outlined the same problems that Jane had and added that the students used the class breaks for "bitter complaint" and that they were "terrified" about how the class would finish.

Dean Smith sighed as she dropped the letter on her crowded desk. Clearly, there would be no easy answers to this problem.

Dean Smith thought back to her hiring of Jennifer Noonan. She remembered her as an intense young woman who had a BA with honors from a small but prestigious liberal arts college, an MA from the other major research institution in town, and most of the work completed for her Ph.D. Although this course topic was not her specialty, she'd been thrilled to fill in when the original teacher canceled. She was very eager to teach and she'd spent the better part of the summer planning the course.

The dean called and left a message asking Jennifer to come in to talk about her course and then called the faculty development coordinator, Chuck Granzow.

Chuck already knew Jennifer and had been working with her in a small reflective practice group. She had been one of the first to sign up for the program and seemed to take it quite seriously. She had expressed some frustration to him about the way the course was going and about an apparent strong clash in expectations. He observed that there seemed to be a lack of trust between the students and Jennifer and that it might be reassuring to the class to have outside intervention. "You might want to suggest to her that I come to her class and do a Small-Group Instructional Diagnosis," he concluded.

By the time a meeting was set, another class period had gone by. Jennifer was shocked and hurt by the strength of the students' dissatisfaction with the course and said that she appreciated the opportunity for guidance. She too was frustrated.

"I've found the students to be less prepared and less uniform in their preparations than I expected, certainly less prepared than I was as an undergraduate. You told me to expect that many of the students would have degrees and be looking ahead to graduate work in psychology. That's true, but there are still many who don't have disciplined study habits. I don't think it's unreasonable to expect students to read articles several times and outline them. I'm not, however, going to distribute vocabulary lists to an upper-level course. When I pressed them to come up with the words they didn't understand, they could only come up with 'intraorganismic' and 'antecedents.'

"I tried to be accurate in my course description by calling the course a theory course, but I think they expected more clinical examples. That will come in the latter half of the course, but now they have to understand the competing theories before we try to apply them."

Jennifer acknowledged that she might have been defensive at times, but she was striving to overcome it. "One woman in the class is stirring up trouble. She's even giving out your cards and urging people to call you. I feel really undercut." There was a quiver in her voice and she paused and took a breath.

"But it's only a vocal minority who object. Mary Lou Gates called me after class to express her support. Maybe you should get her impression.

"Anyway, I think we now have things worked out. We had another discussion about how the class was going. I took a lot of heat, but the class agreed to a new format: each student will sign up to make a ten minute presentation on one of the readings and to include questions for class discussion. After each presentation, I will make summary remarks, highlighting any part of the article which I think may have been omitted or which needed more emphasis. I asked for a show of hands, and people indicated that this would be agreeable. I want to do a good job here," she said intently.

Dean Smith felt reassured. She told Jennifer that she had been intending to recommend that she have Chuck Granzow come to her class for a diagnostic session. Now she did not feel the need so urgently, but asked Jennifer to discuss the idea with Chuck at their next session. She also asked Jennifer to check back with her in several weeks to report on how the course was going. Jennifer left, thanking her for the help.

Dean Smith called Mary Lou Gates, who said that many of the articles were very difficult and that they, and Jennifer's expectations about the course, seemed to be at a graduate level. She said that Jennifer agreed to their "bottom line" that they needed synopses of the articles, and had great respect for Jennifer's willingness to allow time for students to complain about the course not once but twice. She said that she felt some of the students were hostile and rude, but felt optimistic that the course was now on the right track.

Chuck and Jennifer decided that it would be wise to videotape a portion of the class so that they could analyze it together. Chuck arranged for the taping of the next week's session.

Dean Smith also called another student she knew in the class, Denise Farrell, a member of the Student Advisory Board. She asked her, neutrally, how her semester was going. "Fine," she replied, "except for a problem with my psychology class. It's been a problem because the teacher won't lecture. Now, suddenly this week, someone shows up to tape the class and she gives a good lecture. But as soon as the videotaper leaves, the class disintegrates. Plus, she's sort of stuck up. Our copy packet refers to her as 'Professor Noonan,' but we all know she's just a graduate student." Dean Smith pointed out that "Professor" was the convention used by the copy shop and promised to look into the situation.

Again, Jennifer was shocked to hear that students were still unhappy. She insisted that she had told them that she was taping the class to learn more about her teaching and was hurt that they perceived her to be playing to the camera. Clearly, she was trying hard to fix things.

Nonetheless, phone calls continued to come in regarding the class. Students petitioned to withdraw and receive tuition refunds. Yet Jennifer continued to work with Chuck and to insist that the class was improving and that Dean Smith was not hearing from the silent majority. When the students objected that the take-home midterm was too difficult, Jennifer had another faculty member look it over. He concurred, and the following week she split the exam in two and gave only a portion of it. Then a student called, irate because he had taken two days off work to write the exam, only to learn that he did twice the necessary work. Wearily, Dean Smith established a meeting with Jennifer Noonan and Chuck Granzow later that week.

In the meantime, Denise Farrell had taken to dropping in for an update on how fixing their class was going. She said that other students were looking to her, as a Student Advisory Board member, for information. The first time or two, Dean Smith would tell her that the midterm would be revised or that a meeting had been established. Finally, she began to feel that the lines of communication had been seriously tangled. "Please don't keep asking me that question," she said earnestly, but with some frustration. "The answer should be visible in your class itself."

Denise looked taken aback and seemed to wonder what had happened to the open door policy. Who would advocate for the students in the class if not the dean in charge of the department?

After she left, Dean Smith slumped back in her chair. When she spoke with Jennifer, she believed that the class was improving. The reports from students indicated it was not. She had heard from a third of the class by that point and it was now ten weeks into the semester. Where did the truth lie? How could she get at it without undercutting the teacher or forfeiting her own credibility with students as an advocate on their behalf?

Part Two

It was early in the spring semester when a thick packet of teacher evaluation summaries appeared on Assistant Dean Margaret Smith's desk. Every semester, students in each University College course were asked to evaluate the teacher and the course using a standard form. Half of the form asked for student response on a five point scale to statements such as "The instructor communicated ideas in a clear and organized manner." The other half asked for narrative responses to open questions such as the most valuable aspect of the course. A central office within the university collated the responses and produced summary pages. They always made informative reading.

Dean Smith was especially eager to receive this batch. The preceding semester had included a course with the most troublesome clash of student and faculty expectations that she had ever encountered. The instructor made repeated earnest efforts to respond to the class's dissatisfaction and each time believed she had resolved the issues to the satisfaction of the majority; the students (or at least a small but vocal group of them) continued to raise objections. The conundrum was in determining where the truth lay.

The summary page indicated that responses had been obtained from sixteen of the twenty-six students initially enrolled in the class. Only 6% agreed that the instructor communicated ideas in a clear and organized manner. Twenty-five percent remained neutral and 68% disagreed or disagreed strongly. However, 25% believed that the instructor was well prepared for class and 56% judged the time spent on readings and assignments to be worthwhile. Only 12% believed that the course was taught at an appropriate level. It seemed clear that the majority of the students had not had a good experience in this class.

At that moment the phone rang. It was Jennifer Noonan, the instructor in question.

"Hi, Dean Smith," she began brightly. "I'm calling because I'd like to propose a new course to teach for your program next year. It may be pitched a little high for your undergraduates, but I think I could make it work. Can we talk about it?"

Dean Smith winced, but she realized that Jennifer could not yet have received the instructor's copy of the evaluations.

"Jennifer, I was just looking at the summary of your class's evaluation forms. You should be receiving it shortly in the mail. I'm afraid that they don't bear out your sense that the majority of the students were happy with the course. The numbers indicate quite the reverse. I know you tried hard to improve the course, but I don't anticipate hiring you to teach for us again."

There was a long pause. "I know I got off on the wrong foot, but I'd like to try again. Are they that bad?"

"Well, as a matter of fact, they are. I believe that you can learn to be an effective teacher, but I don't think you can do so here. There was a lot of word-of-mouth about the difficulties in your course circulating among the student body last semester. Many of our students consult the evaluation summary book before signing up for courses. Between those two things, your reputation as a teacher at this school is irreparably damaged. I don't believe you would get enough enrollment for the course to run."

At that, a note of concern crept into Jennifer's voice. "Where are these summaries published? Does the chair of my committee get a copy?"

Dean Smith explained that the summaries were available for student review in each University College office, with each UC academic adviser, and in each campus's library. Copies were not ordinarily sent to committee chairs. She indicated that she did not see the need to do so.

"Well, Dean Smith, since you've made it clear that you

won't be hiring me again, I'd like to ask you to suppress my course evaluation summary. After all, if they exist to provide information to students choosing their teachers for future semesters and I'm not going to teach, why should my summary remain available? It would be painful to me and of no use to them."

Now it was Dean Smith's turn to pause. This was another first. What should she do?

In the end, Dean Smith conferred with her colleagues. They decided that the evaluation summaries existed for two reasons. The primary one was to provide information to students who were selecting future courses and instructors. The second, however, was to allow each student a voice in responding to a course and teacher. Suppressing the harsh evaluation would be silencing the students who completed the course and who might wish to read the summary to see how their fellows reacted to the course. Therefore, they decided not to suppress the evaluations.

Questions:
1. Describe what's happening here: who are the main characters and what do we know about them?
2. This seems to be a case of a "clash of expectations." Who expected what? How can this kind of clash be avoided?
3. What could Jennifer, the instructor, have done differently? Dean Smith? The students?

The Purloined Letter
Louise Love

"I need to talk to you." An uneasy voice was recorded on the voicemail. "One of my students turned in a paper that wasn't all his own work, and I'm not sure what I should do. I understand that you deal with academic dishonesty. Please call me as soon as you can. I don't know what I should say to the student in class tonight if he asks me about his paper."

The voice was that of a new teacher—new to this college within the university, at least. She was an investments counsellor who had taught part-time in various schools around the city for a number of years. The course—Corporate Finance.

Associate Dean Winston Witter received the message. "Not another," he groaned. "This must be the Year of the Plagiarist." Three other suspected cases of plagiarism had been brought to his attention that year. Witter had been appalled at the brazenness of the plagiarists and the blatancy of the crimes—nor did he miss their ironies. The first plagiarist had simply shortened and rearranged the Cliff's Notes on Aristotle's *Nicomachean Ethics*. "Ethics, indeed!" Witter had snorted. The second plagiarist copied word-for-word an article on teen-age plastic surgery from the issue of *Cosmopolitan* that was currently on the stands. "How sad," Witter had sneered, "for one to wish to be that which one is not." It had annoyed him that the number two plagiarist had not even gone to the trouble of getting a back issue. Number three plagiarist had simply stolen ("kidnapped" to be etymologically correct) his "research paper" from an obscure but scholarly economics journal (the source had been easily located by the teacher using electronic "searching"). The irony in this case was the third plagiarist's failure to acknowledge not only the author of the article but also the 167 footnotes that the real author had conscientiously included in the ten-page article. All three of these suspected plagiarists had been found guilty by Dean Witter and dismissed from the university.

Fed up with these offenses, Witter had decided to write a letter to all registered students at the beginning of the semester alerting them to the hard line the administration had taken on recent cases of academic dishonesty. He had written the letter because he believed that this kind of information was not likely to be common knowledge among the students. The "perps" who were dismissed from the university for academic dishonesty were not about to let the other students know about the status of crime and punishment at the college. Curiously, Witter's letter had triggered some very anxious phone calls from students who had somehow gotten the idea that the letter was aimed at them personally. But that is another story.

* * * * *

"Ponnie, this is Win Witter." After several tries, Witter was able to reach the teacher. "I got your message. What has Number Four lifted?"

"Thanks for calling, Win. What do you mean 'number four'? I called you about a student in my class named Sam Kinski. Actually, I think he's a full-time day student in the School of Music. He has mentioned to the class that he is a musician and has handed out flyers from a couple of gigs he's done in Chicago. Anyway, I asked the class to write a five-to-seven-page paper on the financial status of a corporation. They could choose any company they were interested in. I asked them to turn in the company's annual report with their paper, but I think I said something to the effect that I would not be reading the annual reports. Or that I probably would not have time to read the annual reports. Or, you know, something like that. But, of course, I *did* read the annual report, or part of it, in some cases, and that's when I discovered where Sam got most of his paper. There was a letter to the stockholders from the company's CEO at the beginning of the annual report. Three pages of

Sam's six-page paper were copied from that letter. The only change he made was, where the CEO wrote 'I' or 'we,' Sam changed it to 'they.' In some of the schools I've taught in, a student caught copying like this can simply do another assignment and substitute it for the first paper. Maybe he would lose a few points for turning the assignment in late. Frankly, I think I should fail him for the assignment and not give him a chance to do another, but that's why I wanted to check with you. Do you think he should be able to write a replacement paper? Or, should the 'F' just get averaged in with his other grades?"

"Well, Ponnie," Witter was always amazed at the contempt that plagiarists show for their teachers, "there may be more consequences for Sam than just an 'F' for the paper. This sounds pretty blatant to me. You may not be aware of this, but we have a very low tolerance for plagiarism around here. As a rule, the student will fail the assignment, fail the course, and be expelled from the university. I'll have to check to see what jurisdiction the School of Music may have in this instance—if, in fact, the student is enrolled there and not with us. When you see Sam in class tonight, just tell him that you suspect that a breach of academic integrity may have occurred and tell him that I will be in touch with him soon to set up an appointment. Just be careful not to say anything that suggests that he has already been 'convicted.' He has to have an opportunity to explain what happened before a final judgment is made."

"Thanks, Win, I'm very upset about this. There are also some other things in his paper that are not actually his own ideas or words. Do you want me to send you a copy of the paper and the annual report?"

"Please do," sighed Witter. "Highlight anything that you think is not the student's own writing. I'll call you if I have any questions."

* * * * *

Witter wrote the mandatory letter to the student asking him to call for an appointment to discuss an alleged breach of academic integrity. The letter named plagiarism as the particular "breach" and stated that the consequences, should the allegation prove true, could include failure of the assignment, failure of the course, and dismissal from the university.

Meanwhile, Witter determined that Sam was, in fact, a full-time student carrying more than a full-time load. He was registered for four day classes in the School of Music as well as his one evening class in corporate finance. Witter called his counterpart in the School of Music to decide how to proceed. They agreed that jurisdiction over the course belonged to the college and that jurisdiction over the student's status in the university belonged to the School of Music.

"I don't know how lenient you are on plagiarism cases," Witter told his colleague, "but if this were a student in the college, he'd be out the door! I'll let you know what happens."

When the package arrived, Dean Witter read the the student's paper, the annual report of the Puella Pulchra Corporation (PPC), and the notes written by Ponnie Manzafrodakis. In the opening paragraph of the paper, Kinski (or Number Four, as Witter thought of him) had stated that the CEO of PPC was confident that the corporation was in a solid financial posture. He then went on to make the same points as those in the CEO's letter and to support the points with data drawn from the later pages of the report. In the next section he presented some general principles on how corporations evaluate their financial positions and named three of the models that may be used to predict future growth. He then brought those models to bear on potential for future growth of PPC and closed with an optimistic statement about the growth potential of PPC. The closing was essentially a paraphrase of the final statement in the CEO's letter. In this section, the student had changed the pronouns from "we" to "they."

Manzafrodakis's notes explained that the three models

detailed in the paper had been presented in several lectures in her class. She wrote that the only original work in Kinski's paper was the application of these models to the specific situation of PPC. Everything else, she felt, was either hers or the CEO's—neither properly acknowledged.

Witter was a little surprised that this paper did not have the long passages of word-for-word copying that he had seen in other cases. But there was plenty of borrowing.

* * * * *

The following week, Sam arrived to meet with Dean Witter. "Good to meet you, Dean. I want to get this misunderstanding cleared up. You know I'm graduating in June. I'm not even in your school. I just wanted to learn something about business so I can manage my career as a performer. I've been taking business courses all along—Accounting, Business Law, Marketing. Very good courses, too. I've enjoyed my experience in the night school."

"Sam," Witter was all business. He had a reverse reaction to being buttered up. "You turned in a six-page paper in your Corporate Finance class. Almost half of the paper was paraphrased from a letter in the published annual report. And in some places you used the exact words and phrases of the CEO."

"I know that I agreed with a lot of what the CEO said, but I put his name right in the first paragraph. I thought I made it clear that I was pretty much agreeing with him. I didn't use quotation marks because I put almost everything in my own words, but I thought I made it clear up front that I was getting my opinion from him and the annual report. Where else would I get my opinion from? I even turned in the report with the paper!"

Kinski shifted to a different subject, "Listen, I went to excellent private schools before I came here. I know all about these things. My prep school was probably the best in the country. I realize now that I should have been more careful about paraphrasing and using quotation marks, but I was in a big hurry because of all my other classes and some gigs I was doing. I'll be happy to put the quotation marks in now or, if you want me to, I'll even write another paper with more quotation marks and footnotes. That would be no problem for me. Believe me, I know how to do this. I just got sloppy because I was in a hurry. And I've learned something from this experience. I'm not a bad person."

"We're not here to make judgments about what kind of a person you are." Witter wanted to keep the conversation focused. "Tell me, though, if you thought you had acknowledged the CEO's ideas in the paper, why did you change the pronouns in the last paragraph?"

"You *can* change words in quoted material. I checked." Kinski was shifting ground again. "I just should have put those words in brackets. I admit I should have done that. And, as I said, I'll be happy to do it now. I'll do whatever you think is best. I just don't want my father to know about this. He's a big donor, you know. I'm afraid the president would be really upset if something unfair happened to me."

"Sam, your paragraphs on models for future growth were taken directly from the Professor Manzafrodakis's lectures. Those lectures should be acknowledged in your paper. One of your sentences is a word-for-word quote from a lecture. That's like stealing your teacher's words, isn't it?"

Genuine dismay registered on Kinski's face. "You mean I'm supposed to mention the lectures I took notes on? I took that information right out of my class notes. How am I supposed to remember which ones were her words? I mean isn't that what I'm taking the class for—to learn some new stuff that I didn't know before? That's not a crime, is it?"

Witter continued, "Do you know I wrote a letter to every student registered in the college at the beginning of the semester reminding them of the importance of academic integrity and warning them about the kinds of sanctions that can be imposed when a student violates it. In the letter I said that if you are unsure about what constitutes plagiarism, you can pick up a copy of a document called *Plagia-*

rism and How to Avoid It in the office. Did you get a copy of this letter?"

"Not that I recall, but I might have. I get a lot of mail because, you know, I'm running a music business on the side. But, I don't think I got your letter. Anyway, it doesn't apply to me because I didn't do anything dishonest. I just took the material that I had studied and brought it together. I knew the teacher would know where I got the models. I figured she'd be happy to see that I took notes and learned them. What more can I do? If you say I should have mentioned the lectures, I'll redo the paper. I honestly had no idea that you were supposed to do that. And another thing. I've never had to write a paper like this before. You can check my record. I've been taking performance classes and business and math and things like that that don't require papers. Now I've learned what I need to do. Listen, it would really upset my dad if this hurt my chances of getting into law school."

Witter did not respond well to veiled threats. "I have to conclude that this copying of someone else's words and ideas was done intentionally with an intent to deceive. The changing of the pronouns convinces me of that."

"You were convinced before I walked in the door," Sam was warming to the indignity. "Do you really think I'm so stupid that I would turn in the annual report with the paper if I meant to deceive?"

Witter had seen "trapped" plagiarists go from deferential to aggressive before. "I have to conclude that you took Professor Manzafrodakis at her word when she told the class she would not read the annual reports. I will write to you with my final decision, but at this moment I believe you will fail the assignment and the course. Any change in your status at the university will be decided by your home school."

"I did not get a fair hearing." Kinski was shaken. "This meeting was a farce. You decided what you were going to do before I even came in here. I'm going to take this over your head. This is totally unfair."

Kinski left the office murmuring threats about taking

this injustice to the president of the university. Dean Witter checked Kinski's transcript to see if, in fact, he had taken other courses that might have required a research paper. And, as the student had stated, his courses had been almost entirely performance courses and business courses. His grades were good. "I wonder how he got the rest of his grades," Witter muttered to himself.

Kinski failed the assignment and the course. Witter told this to the associate dean in the School of Music and told her again that the college would dismiss such a student.

The School of Music asked Kinski to write a paper on proper forms of attribution. He graduated in June.

Questions:
1. Should the instructor have handled this differently?
2. Did the dean overreact?
3. Should the student have a chance to rewrite?
4. Are there degrees of plagiarism?
5. What is an appropriate measure of discipline in a case which might as easily be honest error as intentional misconduct?

The Art and Science of Teaching the Arts and Sciences: The Case of the New Faculty Developer

Regina Lopata Logan

Martha Bowers was not a newcomer to academics. In fact, she had been involved in adult education and administration for more than twenty years. However, she had "stopped out" during the last few years to have her family and complete her Ph.D. Her dissertation, freshly minted, was on adult development, and she had earned a master's degree in adult education about ten years previously. She had not really been actively looking for a job, primarily because she wanted to be home with her three school-aged children. However, when the opportunity for a part time position as Coordinator of Faculty Development for the evening division of a prestigious university came her way, she seized it with gusto.

One of the things Martha loved about her new job was the creativity and freedom it afforded her. The existing faculty development program had been quite successful but she felt it needed some different approaches. Her ideas met with success, both from faculty and administrators, until one day... .

Martha had revamped a series of workshops for new faculty. Her predecessor, who had a Ph.D. in adult learning and seemed very experienced to Martha, had relied heavily on experiential learning in the development program. Martha, too, strongly believed in interactive learning. However, she felt there had been too much emphasis placed on "reflective practice" (jargon that she had recently picked up) and not enough focus on the "nuts and bolts" of teaching. Thus, she created a series of workshops that included topics such as syllabus writing, lecturing, discussion, and grading. The workshops were well attended (at least twenty-five faculty came to each offering), and each workshop was held twice. Of course, the fact that there was an incentive of $350 awarded to any instructor who attended five workshops certainly didn't hurt the attendance!

The first two workshops seemed to go quite well. However, she still didn't feel an "expert" in the field, especially compared to Will, her highly regarded predecessor. She just hoped no one would ask her too many questions she couldn't answer. She knew she understood adult development, but she was still uneasy about whether she really knew enough of the literature in adult learning to pass herself off as a "faculty developer." Yet her evaluations had been encouraging, and the dean seemed satisfied with her work. On a bright autumn day, her confidence growing, she entered the large meeting room to begin the third in the workshop series: "Enhancing Participation."

When the workshops were taught in the evening, there was a range of faculty present: professionals in the community, instructors at her university who also taught in the day school, and faculty from other institutions. In the daytime workshops such as this, the participants were almost exclusively advanced doctoral students. Many of them had experience as teaching assistants, and some had taught their own classes, but for the most part they were teaching their own classes for the first time. Few had ever taught adults before.

After welcoming them and leading some general discussion on student participation and methods of interactive learning, Martha followed her plan to break into small groups. The participants self-selected into groups of five to seven. Because many of them were already seated with their departmental colleagues, the groups fell somewhat naturally into disciplines. Martha gave the groups the task of brainstorming kinds of participatory learning exercises and discussing what they thought were the pros and cons of each.

All the groups seemed to get off to an energetic start. The social science group was having a heated debate over the utility of case studies; the humanities people were thoughtfully engaged in conversation about group projects; in the fine arts and music faculty group, each person presented ideas for giving feedback on original works of art; the math, economics, and computer science instructors, in one group, and the sciences faculties, in another group, were taking turns presenting their points of view to their colleagues. Martha floated around the room, hovering on the periphery of each group, enjoying their different styles and interests. She was feeling pleased with herself; without being smug, she felt she had brought her imprimatur to the Faculty Development Program, revitalizing it and meeting the faculty's needs in a direct way.

Suddenly she was startled out of her reflection by the sheer silence in two areas of the large meeting room. The math group and the sciences group were both just sitting there. She had given the groups ten to fifteen minutes for this exercise. Only three or four minutes had elapsed. She walked uneasily over to the math/computer science group. Her own academic background, both undergraduate and graduate, had been almost exclusively in the social sciences and humanities. She always felt a little intimidated by the harder-edged disciplines. As she approached them, Henry, obviously the group's spokesperson, looked up at her, with a distinctly bored expression on his face.

"Have you each had an opportunity to share?" Martha asked.

"Well, we really didn't have that much to '*share*,'" Henry replied, with what Martha was certain was a sarcastic emphasis on 'share.'

"Yes," Lu Chen agreed softly, "it's pretty straightforward for us."

Martha queried the group, "You mean, you all feel comfortable about how to encourage students to participate?"

Again, Henry spoke, in a voice that sounded slightly hostile to Martha, "Math is math. You give problems. The students do them. You work your way through the text. You have a weekly quiz. That's it."

Martha was silent, as she could think of no immediate question to ask. Her own anxiety was mounting; without an intuitive sense for their disciplines, no probing questions or examples immediately came to mind. While she was hesitating, she noticed that the sciences group, about fifteen feet away, were listening to her conversation with the math group. She brought them into the conversation, saying, "I see you're finished with this exercise, too. Does it seem pretty much a non-issue for you, too?" Several nodded their heads.

Alicia spoke, "We're so busy with labs and trying to cram all this material into such a short semester that we don't have the luxury of group projects, or even papers, for that matter. Our students are primarily pre-med. They are very focused on covering the topics necessary to prepare for the MCATs and they seem to resent any discussion, even if they have relevant backgrounds. I know that one of my students is a pharmacology technician and two others are nurses. But when I asked them a little about their work, the other students were audibly and visibly hostile; they didn't want to waste any class time on anything but the essentials. So, I teach my biology class geared to the text and design the labs to cram in everything I can."

At least Alicia seemed to understand Martha's desire to have them consider how varying teaching methods might add a dimension of richness to the classroom, especially with adult students.

Henry, however, was altogether a different case. "Yeah, well, our students are so busy with their jobs, and most of them are already into programming, that they just want the next step. And that's what we give them. We really don't have time for much extraneous garbage. We lecture, they listen. There's really no other way to teach our subjects. Now, those guys over there," he gestured to the social sciences and humanities groups, who were still actively involved, "those courses have lots of flexibility and soft stuff and opinions....we don't. And that's about it."

Martha searched her mind for an appropriate comeback. "Well," she began hesitatingly, "maybe it doesn't have to be that way....Maybe you could approach your courses in a fresh, creative way....What do you think?"

Henry rolled his eyes and then shot back, "Give me a break! That...that 'role play' stuff is just a bunch of crap. And these workshops are pretty useless, too. If it weren't for the 350 bucks, none of us would even be here."

Martha's heart raced; her face flushed red and hot. She felt like she had been personally attacked. She took a deep breath and searched the two groups for someone—anyone— who might act as her ally. At the same instant, she noticed that the conversation had begun to die down in the other groups. She had to attend to them before she lost them, too. She looked straight at Henry and said with as firm a voice as she could muster, "I'm sorry you feel that way. Maybe we could think of some ways to make the program more relevant for all the disciplines."

She turned away and moved toward the center of the room. Fighting to regain her composure, she announced, "Let's get back into the big group, now." Her stomach was churning as she suggested, "maybe we can learn something from each other."

Questions:
1. How else could this workshop topic be organized?
2. How can faculty be persuaded to try new teaching methods?
3. What ways can faculty from different disciplines learn about pedagogy from each other?

About the Authors

The Editors

Regina Lopata Logan has been teaching for and about adult learners for more than 25 years. She has taught in both academic and nonacademic environments. She received a Bachelor of Arts degree from the University of Michigan, a Master of Arts degree from the University of Wisconsin in French Language and Literature, a Master of Arts degree in Teaching and Learning Processes, specializing in adult learning, from Northwestern University, and a Doctor of Philosophy degree in Human Development and Social Policy from Northwestern University. She has published in *Psychology and Aging* and *the Journal of Cross-Cultural Psychology*. She has also presented at the Chicago Area Faculty Developers Network, Northwestern University Women in Leadership, the Professional and Organizational Development Network in Higher Education, the Association of Northwestern University Women, and the Society for Research in Child Development. Currently, she is the Director of Faculty Development and a lecturer in Organization Development and Women's Studies at Northwestern University's University College.

Robert M. Fromberg has been a lecturer in English at Northwestern University's University College for the past ten years. Previously he taught at Duke University's continuing education program. He has published more than two dozen short stories in literary magazines, numerous books and articles on health care issues, and a novella entitled Blue Skies. He has a Master of Fine Arts degree in creative writing.

The Contributors

Don Collins, M.A., is Dean Emeritus, Division of Continuing Education, Northwestern University, Evanston, Illinois.

Sandra N. Basile received her B.Phil. in 1996 from University College, Northwestern University. She is currently Assistant Credit Manager, Unimast Incorporated, Schiller Park, Illinois.

Kurt D. Cogswell, Ph.D., is Assistant Professor of Mathematics, South Dakota State University, Brookings, South Dakota.

Leslie A. Fischer, M.A., is Lecturer, University College, Northwestern University, Chicago, Illinois, and Lecturer, Engineering Design and Communication Program, Northwestern University, Evanston, Illinois.

Cecilia M. Germaine received a B.S.G.S. in 1995 from University College, Northwestern University. She is presently Administrative Services Coordinator, Northwestern University Weinberg College of Arts & Sciences, Evanston, Illinois.

Mary Hanson Harrison, Ph.D., is an Adjunct Faculty at Des Moines Area Community College, Des Moines, Iowa.

Carlissa R. Hughes, Ph.D., is a Clinical Psychologist in Chicago, Illinois.

Pat Hutchings, Ph.D., is Senior Scholar, The Carnegie Foundation for the Advancement of Teaching, Menlo Park, California.

John Jacob, Ph.D., is Lecturer, University College, Northwestern University Chicago, Illinois.

Louise Love, Ph.D., is Vice Dean, Division of Continuing Education, Northwestern University, Chicago, Illinois.

Andra Medea, M.A., is employed by Medea & Associates, Inc., Chicago, Illinois.

Barbara J. Millis, Ph.D., is Director, Faculty Development, U. S. Air Force Academy, Colorado Springs, Colorado.

James R. O'Laughlin, M.A., is Lecturer, University College and The Writing Program, Northwestern University, Evanston, Illinois.

Gary L. Phillips, S.T.D., is Lecturer, University College, Northwestern University, Chicago/Evanston, Illinois; Associate Core Faculty, Illinois School of Professional Psychology, Chicago, Illinois; and Adjunct Faculty, Garrett Evangelical Theological Seminary, Evanston.

Joan Hattstrom-Phillips, M.S.W., is a Clinical Social Worker, Lecturer, and Consultant in Chicago, Illinois.

Lydia J. Rohn, received a B.S.G.S. in 1996 from University College, Northwestern University. She is Senior Human Resource Consultant, McGladrey & Pullen, LLP, Schaumburg, Illinois.

Laurence D. Schiller, Ph.D., is Lecturer, Department of History, and Head Fencing Coach, Northwestern University, Evanston, Illinois.

Hilary Ward Schnadt, Ph.D., is Associate Dean, University College, Northwestern University, Chicago, Illinois.